F-15 Eagle
in action

By Al Adcock

Color by Don Greer

Illustrated by John Lowe and Richard Hudson

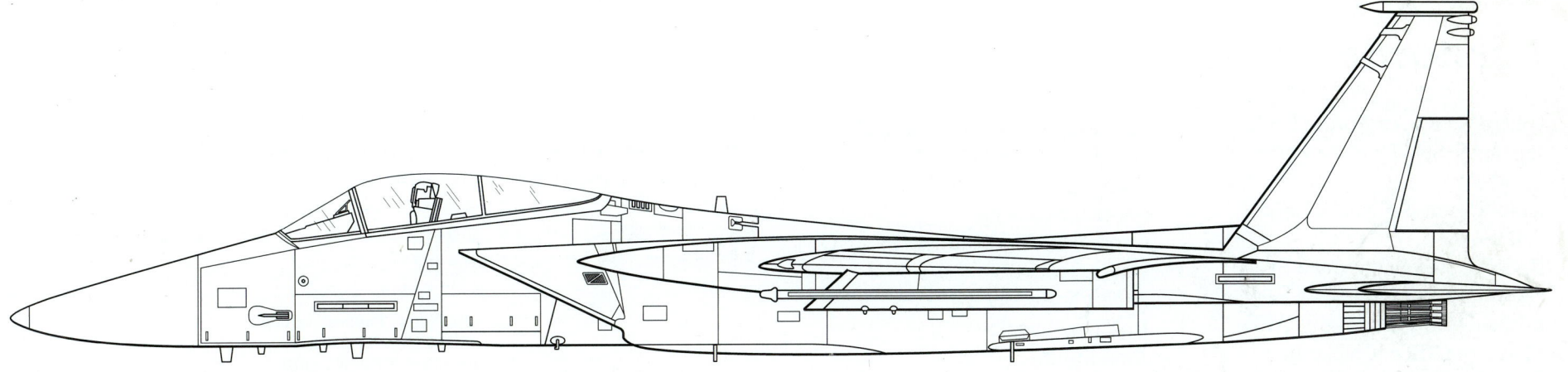

Aircraft Number 183

squadron/signal publications

Capt Jay T. Denney flew this F-15C Eagle (84-0025) when he downed two Iraqi MiG-23s over central Iraq on 27 January 1991. Denney was assigned to the 53rd Tactical Fighter Squadron (TFS), 36th Tactical Fighter Wing (TFW) during Operation DESERT STORM. The Wing deployed from Bitburg Air Base (AB), Germany to Incirlik AB, Turkey for the US-led Coalition effort against Iraq.

Acknowledgements

United States Air Force (USAF)
Japan Air Self-Defense Force (JASDF)
Israel Defense Force/Air Force (IDF/AF)
National Aeronautics and Space Administration (NASA)
Edwards Air Force Base (AFB) History Office, California
Raymond L. Puffer, Ph.D.
McDonnell Douglas
Boeing
Todd Blecher
33rd Fighter Wing, Eglin AFB, Florida
325th Fighter Wing, Tyndall AFB, Florida
125th Fighter Wing, Florida Air National Guard (FLANG)
TSgt Fernando Serna, USAF
Airman Magazine
Captain Richard Bittner (FLANG)
David Sconyers
Albert F. Adcock IV
Rob Braithwaite
John Smith
MSgt Joe Sadler, USAF Retired
Chris Smallenberg
General Dynamics
Terry Love
Norris Graser
Bert Kinzey, Detail & Scale, Inc.
Lou Drendel
Centurion Enterprises

COPYRIGHT 2002 SQUADRON/SIGNAL PUBLICATIONS, INC.
1115 CROWLEY DRIVE CARROLLTON, TEXAS 75011-5010
All rights reserved. No part of this publication may be reproduced, stored in a retrieval system or transmitted in any form by means electrical, mechanical or otherwise, without written permission of the publisher.

ISBN 0-89747-445-7

If you have any photographs of aircraft, armor, soldiers or ships of any nation, particularly wartime snapshots, why not share them with us and help make Squadron/Signal's books all the more interesting and complete in the future. Any photograph sent to us will be copied and the original returned. The donor will be fully credited for any photos used. Please send them to:

Squadron/Signal Publications, Inc.
1115 Crowley Drive
Carrollton, TX 75011-5010

Если у вас есть фотографии самолётов, вооружения, солдат или кораблей любой страны, особенно, снимки времён войны, поделитесь с нами и помогите сделать новые книги издательства Эскадрон/Сигнал ещё интереснее. Мы переснимем ваши фотографии и вернём оригиналы. Имена приславших снимки будут сопровождать все опубликованные фотографии. Пожалуйста, присылайте фотографии по адресу:

Squadron/Signal Publications, Inc.
1115 Crowley Drive
Carrollton, TX 75011-5010

軍用機、装甲車両、兵士、軍艦などの写真を所持しておられる方はいらっしゃいませんか？どの国のものでも結構です。作戦中に撮影されたものが特に良いのです。Squadron/Signal社の出版する刊行物において、このような写真は内容を一層充実し、興味深くすることができます。当方にお送り頂いた写真は、複写の後お返しいたします。出版物中に写真を使用した場合は、必ず提供者のお名前を明記させて頂きます。お写真は下記にご送付ください。

Squadron/Signal Publications, Inc.
1115 Crowley Drive
Carrollton, TX 75011-5010

(Right) A McDonnell Douglas F-15A-12-MC (74-118) assigned to the Commander of the 325th Fighter Wing (FW) flies over the Florida panhandle in 1992. The Wing is based at Tyndall Air Force Base (AFB), Florida and trains F-15 pilots. The tail band consists of red (top), yellow, and blue stripes. These stripes represent the Wing's 1st Fighter Squadron (FS), 2nd FS, and 95th FS, respectively. Art below the windshield depicts an eagle rendition with the name Panama City – located 12 miles (19.3 км) west of Tyndall AFB. (McDonnell Douglas)

Introduction

The North American Bald Eagle has long been the symbol of freedom and power of the United States of America. It was only fitting when the first McDonnell Douglas **F-15** air superiority fighter rolled off the assembly line in 1972 that it was also named the **Eagle**.

United States Army Air Forces (USAAF) pilots enjoyed air superiority during the Second World War flying the superb North American P-51 Mustang and the stout Republic P-47 Thunderbolt. The Korean War that followed in 1950 again proved the value of 'owning the skies,' when the North American F-86 Sabre gained a 13 to 1 advantage over North Korea's Mikoyan-Gurevich MiG-15, which was sometimes flown by Soviet pilots. Americans were again flying against an enemy air force 15 years later, this time in the unfriendly skies over North Vietnam.

The air superiority that the earlier US pilots enjoyed evaporated when the US Air Force (USAF) and US Navy (USN) came up against the pilots of the Vietnamese People's Air Force flying the MiG-17, MiG-19, and MiG-21. North Vietnam's light, fast, and nimble fighters showed no mercy to the USAF/USN McDonnell Douglas F-4 Phantom, an aircraft designed as a high altitude interceptor and not for close-in dog fighting. The Americans were able to gain only a meager 1.5 to 1 kill ratio over their foes. This was obviously unacceptable to the Admirals and Generals charged with the air defense of American interests.

Air combat over North Vietnam finally resulted in the USAF requesting a study in 1965 for the development of a Fighter Experimental (FX). The FX design eventually led to two Requests For Proposals (RFPs) for a 40,000 pound (18,144 KG) fixed geometry wing design, which led to the F-15 Eagle. During this same time frame, the USN opted for a variable geometry wing design, which resulted in the Grumman F-14 Tomcat. The RFPs resulted in the USAF issuing a Concept Formulation Study (CFS) for the FX in March of 1966.

No less than six manufacturers submitted designs to the USAF within the boundaries of the CFS for the F-15. Grumman, Lockheed, North American Rockwell, General Dynamics, Fairchild Hiller, and McDonnell Douglas all submitted proposals in 1967. The USAF considered all proposals by late 1969 and selected the McDonnell Douglas design for production. The aircraft was ordered from paper designs, with no prototype aircraft built.

On 23 December 1969, the USAF issued a contract for the construction of 107 Full-Scale Development (FSD) single-seat **F-15A** and two-seat **TF-15A** (later designated **F-15B**) aircraft. The F-15 was designed as an air superiority fighter, with a secondary role of ground attack. This aircraft was designed to dominate the skies utilizing its armament of a multi-barreled 20MM General Electric M61A1 Vulcan cannon, four Raytheon AIM-7 Sparrow and four Philco (now Ford Aerospace) AIM-9 Sidewinder Air-to-Air Missiles (AAMs). These weapons could defeat any aerial foe, whether it was a fighter at close range or a high-flying bomber at long range. The F-15 was primarily designed to engage Soviet aircraft – such as the MiG and Sukhoi fighters and the Tupolev and Ilyushin bombers – no matter what air force was operating them. The secondary ground attack role allowed the Eagle to carry up to 9000 pounds (4082.4 KG) of external stores.

The F-15 could carry up to three 600 gallon (2271.2 L) external fuel tanks, which provided an unrefueled range of over 3000 miles (4827.9 KM). This permitted the F-15 to fly non-stop to Europe, which was one of the contract's requirements. The F-15's air-to-air refueling capabilities offer a range limited only by the crew's stamina, usually not over 6000 miles (9655.8 KM). The F-15B (TF-15A) introduced the FAST (Fuel And Sensor Tactical) Pack Conformal Fuel Tanks (CFTs; also called fuel pallets), which are affixed to the sides of the fuselage along the air intake ducts. These pallets each have a capacity of 728 gallons (2755.8 L) of additional fuel.

The F-15 contract called for the construction of 20 pre-production aircraft, with 12 examples going to McDonnell Douglas and the remaining eight to the USAF for evaluation. The first ten

The McDonnell Douglas F-4 Phantom was the premier air superiority fighter both for the US Navy and the US Air Force during the 1960s, until the McDonnell-Douglas F-15 replaced it in USAF service in the 1970s. This F-4C (63-7672) was operated by the 123rd FS 'Red Hawks,' Oregon Air National Guard (ANG). This unit guarded the US West Coast and trained ANG pilots. (McDonnell Douglas)

The first YF-15A-1-MC prototype (71-280) conducts a test flight from Edwards AFB, California in 1972. International Orange (FS12197) recognition panels are painted over the Air Superiority Blue finish (FS35450 over FS15450). An air data probe is mounted on the nose to collect test data. (McDonnell Douglas)

prototype aircraft were single seat YF-15As, assigned the serial numbers 71-280 through 71-289. The number 11 and 12 prototype aircraft were the YTF-15A two-seaters, serialed 71-290 and 71-291. The USAF began receiving their aircraft when they took delivery of the first YF-15A pre-production aircraft, a Block 5 serialed 72-113. Seven prototype aircraft soon followed and flight tests began. The first prototype YF-15A (71-280) made its maiden flight from Edwards Air Force Base (AFB), California on 27 July 1972, with McDonnell Douglas test pilot Irv Burrows at the controls

The YF-15As were powered by two Pratt & Whitney F-100-PW-100 turbofan engines, each producing 14,500 pounds of static thrust and 23,500 pounds of thrust with afterburning. The engine intakes are capable of moving up or down depending on the amount of airflow required by the engines. This airflow amount is determined by the onboard computer and by the Eagle's angle of attack. The afterburning section contained convergent/divergent nozzles, whose actuators were covered by plates nicknamed 'turkey feathers.' These nozzles controlled the thrust by constricting airflow. The YF-15A's maximum rated speed was Mach 2.5 – 1650 MPH (2655.3 KMH) at 36,000 feet (10,972.8 M) – with a nominal cruise speed of Mach 0.9 – 570 MPH (917.3 KMH).

Early in the flight test program, a severe wing buffet problem occurred during flight at Mach 0.9 and 6 Gs.[1] McDonnell Douglas engineers corrected this problem by removing four square feet (0.4 M^2) from each wingtip and this became the standard Eagle wingtip configuration. A dogtooth 16.5 inches (41.9 CM) wide was cut into the horizontal stabilizer's leading edge to correct a mild flutter problem. YF-15s were equipped with a 20 square foot (1.9 M^2) speed brake on the upper fuselage. When it opened at a near vertical angle, this caused a buffet condition at certain airspeeds. This speed brake was enlarged to 31.5 square feet (2.9 M^2) and extended at a smaller angle to eliminate buffeting.

Two years of tests conducted at Edwards AFB, Luke AFB, Arizona, and at the McDonnell

[1] G: Acceleration due to the Earth's gravity. For example, six Gs equal the force of six times the aircraft's weight.

Douglas plant in St. Louis, Missouri revealed no major faults. The only problems concerned a sometimes-faulty engine or some piece of cranky electronic equipment. These were corrected and the USAF ordered series production.

In 1973, a trio of 3/8th-scale polymer and aluminum F-15 models were built to discover the full range of the F-15's flight envelope without putting a pilot at risk. The 2450 pound (1111.3 KG) Remotely Piloted Research Vehicles (RPRVs) were dropped from a National Aeronautics and Space Administration (NASA) NB-52 and flown back to a landing at Edwards AFB. While in flight, the RPRV investigated angles of attack, stall characteristics and spins, and spin recovery. The aircraft landed using a landing gear of sprung skids. A pilot controlled the RPRVs in flight from an exact replica of an F-15 cockpit.

STREAK EAGLE was a USAF attempt to capture various time-to-climb records held by the Soviet MiG-25 (NATO codename Foxbat) and the USN F-4B Phantom. The 17th production, Block 6 F-15A (72-119) was chosen for STREAK EAGLE. All non-essential equipment was removed to save weight, including the 20MM cannon, radar, and most back-up equipment. The paint was removed to save 40 pounds (18.1 KG). The STREAK EAGLE flights were carried out at Grand Forks AFB, North Dakota, to take advantage of cold weather in January and February of 1975. A minimum of fuel was carried, just enough to reach a pre-determined altitude. These flights broke eight existing time-to-climb records, with one record flight that reached 20,000 M (65,616.8 feet) in just 122.94 seconds! For this 19 January 1975 flight, the F-15A weighed 29,877 pounds (13,552.2 KG) and had a power to weight ratio of 1.5 to 1.

The F-15 Eagle scored a series of firsts for a fighter. It was the first fighter aircraft to exceed the speed of sound while in vertical flight, which was made possible by another first of having a thrust-to-weight ratio greater than one to one. The F-15 was the first American fighter to fly non-stop to Europe unrefueled and the first to fly across Australia unrefueled. In the mind of all F-15 pilots, it is their first choice of a fighter in which to go to battle. The F-15 is also the first fighter aircraft in aviation history to shoot down over 95 confirmed enemy aircraft without a single air-to-air loss.

No, NASA is not testing a new landing gear configuration for the F-15. This is a 3/8 scale unpowered model Remotely Piloted Research Vehicle (RPRV) made by McDonnell Douglas from aluminum, fiberglass, and other resins. It was carried to altitude by a NASA Boeing NB-52 and released, then remotely 'flown by a pilot setting in a full-scale replica of an F-15 cockpit. (NASA)

Operation STREAK EAGLE was an F-15A-6-MC (72-119) stripped of all but minimal radio equipment, armament, and paint to reduce weight. It was flown to eight time-to-climb records in 1975. The 17th production Eagle was eventually painted to prevent corrosion and is now displayed at the US Air Force Museum at Wright-Patterson AFB, Ohio. (McDonnell Douglas)

Development

YF-15A Eagle

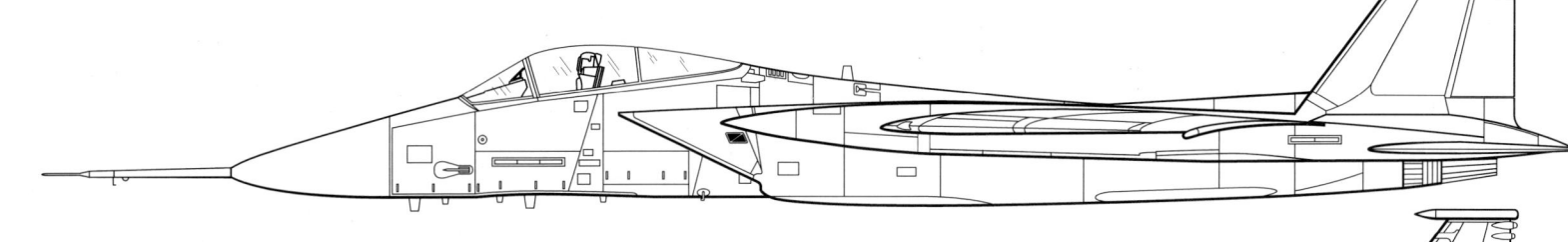

F-15A/C Eagle

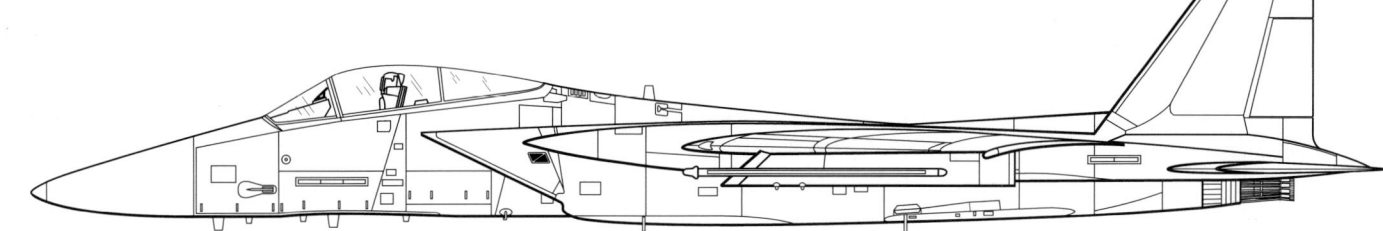

F-15B/D Eagle

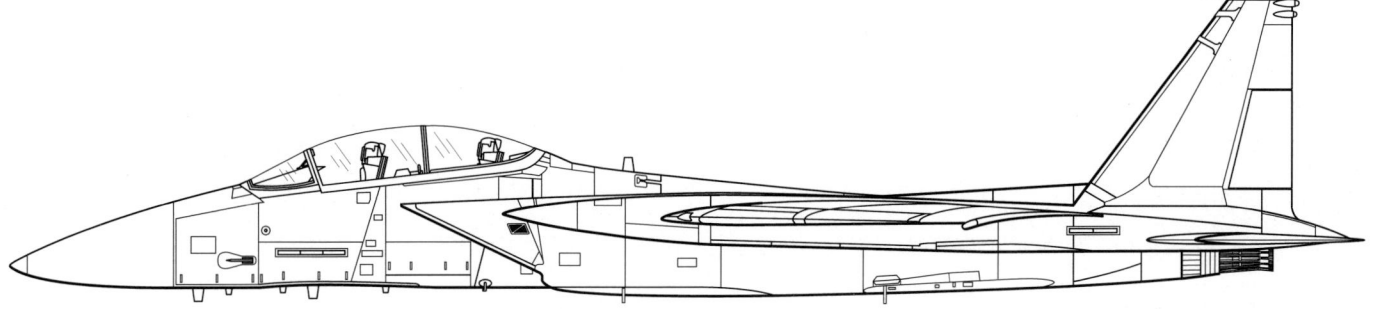

F-15E Eagle

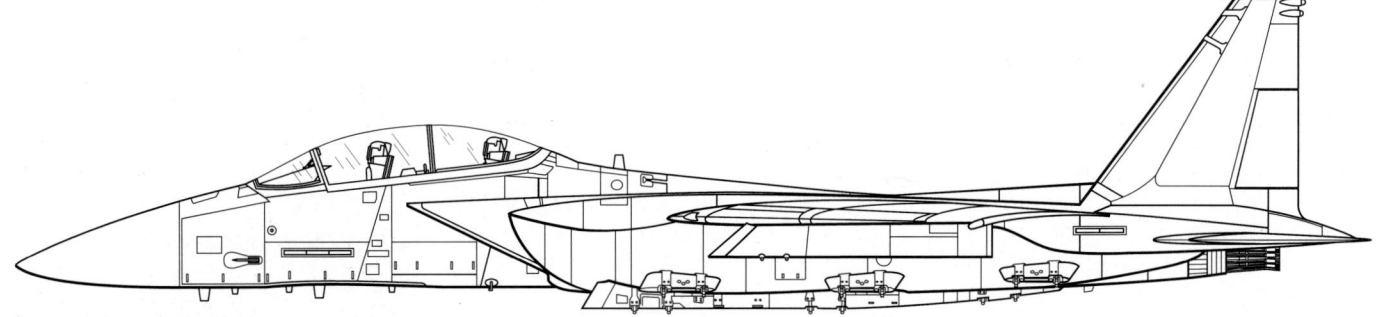

F-15A Eagle

The first of 30 F-15A series production aircraft came off the McDonnell Douglas assembly line in St. Louis in 1973. At that time, the USAF knew it possessed the world's hottest fighter aircraft and they set about training their pilots to utilize this new fighting machine. Luke AFB was chosen to be the training site and the 555th Tactical Fighter Training Squadron (TFTS), the 'Triple Nickel,' was the first Eagle-equipped unit. The 555th TFTS operated the F-15 air superiority fighter until 1989, when they turned their mission over to the 405th Tactical Training Wing (TTW). The 405th was converting to the **F-15E Eagle** dual-role fighter.

The F-15A has a wingspan of 42 feet 9.75 inches (13 M) and a wing area of 608 square feet (56.5 M^2), an overall length of 63 feet 9 inches (19.4 M), and a height of 18 feet 5 1/2 inches (5.6 M). It weighed 27,000 pounds (12,247.2 KG) empty and 66,000 pounds (29,937.6 KG) at take off maximum. This maximum weight is achieved with three 600 gallon (2271.2 L) external fuel tanks – one each on the centerline and under the port and starboard wings – and a full armament of four AIM-7 Sparrow, four AIM-9 Sidewinder AAMs, and 940 rounds for the 20MM M61A1 Vulcan cannon.

Power for the F-15A came from two Pratt & Whitney F-100-PW-100 (USAF designation JTF22A-25A) low bypass axial-flow turbofan engines. Each engine was rated at 12,420 pounds (5634 KG) of static thrust and 23,850 pounds (10,818 KG) of thrust with afterburning. This power gives the F-15A an overall rated speed of 1650 MPH (2655.3 KMH) or Mach 2.5 at 36,000 feet (10,972.8 M) and 975 MPH (1569.1 KMH) at sea level. It has a maximum fuel capacity of 3650 gallons (13,816.7 L), including 1850 gallons (7003 L) of internal fuel and three 600 gallon external fuel tanks. The F-15A with maximum fuel load has an unrefueled range of 3450 miles (5552.1 KM) – a range of approximately one mile (1.6 KM) per gallon (3.8 L).

The F-15's fuselage is built in three sections (front, center, and back) for ease of manufacture. The wings are mounted to the upper fuselage and the leading edges are swept back 45° at the root. Conventional ailerons and flaps are fitted to the trailing edges; however, no leading edge devices are mounted on the wing. The twin vertical stabilizers and both horizontal stabilizers are mounted to the aft fuselage. The Eagle's airframe is primarily metal, with 37.3 percent aluminum, 25.8 percent titanium, and 5.5 percent steel. Composite materials – especially boron-epoxy and honeycomb – are used, primarily on the radome, control surfaces, and vertical tail.

The F-15A is armed with one 20MM M61A1 Vulcan six-barrel rotary cannon, which is mounted in the starboard wing root. The cannon is fed from a 950-round ammunition drum located in the mid-fuselage. The Vulcan can fire up to 6000 rounds per minute and is gyro stabilized for excellent accuracy. The Eagle's external weapons include up to four AIM-7 Sparrow radar-guided AAMs, four AIM-9 Sidewinder infra-red (heat seeking) AAMs, or up to eight Hughes AIM-120 AMRAAMs (Advance Medium Range Air-to-Air Missiles). The AMRAAM is a 'fire and forget' missile, which is guided to its target vicinity by an inertial guidance unit. This unit is data linked to the firing aircraft, ensuring accurate target location. Once acquired, the active seeker directs the missile to its intended aerial target. The AMRAAM began replacing the AIM-7 in the early 1990s and was first used in combat during Operation DESERT STORM against Iraq in early 1991.

The F-15A is primarily an air superiority fighter, but has a secondary air-to-ground capability. Historically, American fighter aircraft have been extensively used in the ground attack role. The P-51 Mustang and the P-47 Thunderbolt were legendary in the ground suppression role

Luke AFB, Arizona was chosen to train F-15 pilots in the 1970s. This F-15A-11-MC (73-103) is assigned to the 461st Tactical Fighter Training Squadron (TFTS)/405th Tactical Training Wing (TTW). It is painted Air Superiority Blue with red and white stripes on the forward fuselage and wings. Yellow and blue squadron colors are painted on the vertical stabilizers. (USAF)

An F-15A-15-MC (76-0022) from the 426th TFTS flies out over the high desert landscape of Arizona in the late 1970s. It is painted in the Compass Ghost Gray scheme of Dark Ghost Gray (FS36320) and Light Ghost Gray (FS36375). The tail band on the vertical stabilizer is red with a yellow jet aircraft. A 600 gallon (2271.2 L) centerline tank is fitted to increase range. (USAF)

This F-15A-14-MC (75-0062) of the 555th TFTS/405th TFTW flies over the Arizona desert in the late 1980s. The 'Triple Nickel' was the first unit equipped with the Eagle and didn't relinquish the air-to-air version until December of 1991. The F-15 is finished in the two-tone Compass Ghost Gray scheme and has a green fin band with five white stars. LA is the tail code for Luke AFB. (USAF)

during the Second World War in the European and Pacific Theatres. During the Vietnam War, the F-4 Phantom was utilized in the air-to-ground role, although it was originally designed for air superiority duties. The ability to operate in either the air-to-air or ground attack roles makes for a most versatile fighter. The F-15A could be armed with up to eighteen 500 pound (226.8 KG) Mk 82 bombs on fuselage and pylon stations using Multiple Ejector Racks (MERs). F-15As can deliver various laser guided weapons, including the GBU-10, GBU-12, GBU-15, and GBU-16; however, these bombs require guidance to the target by a ground or air designator equipped unit.

The centerpiece of the F-15A's avionics equipment is the Hughes AN/APG-63 radar. It is an X-band, almost wholly solid state, Doppler radar with a look-down, shoot-down capability. The AN/APG-63 can locate and identify low flying aerial targets from the ground clutter. It has several air-to-air modes utilizing various pulses for short or long ranges. The radar has a range of over 200 miles (321.9 KM), depending on the F-15A's altitude. A Loral AN/ALR-56C Radar Warning Receiver (RWR) and a Magnavox AN/ALQ-128 Radar Threat Warning System are fitted to detect enemy aerial threats. The AN/ALR-56C's antennas are located on the wingtips and on the front nose gear door, while the AN/ALQ-128 antenna is placed atop the starboard horizontal stabilizer.

The first F-15As were delivered in an overall Air Superiority Blue scheme, which was flat (FS35450) on the upper surfaces and glossy (FS15450) on the undersurfaces. This color scheme camouflaged the Eagle at high altitudes – perhaps camouflaging too well for training. The 555th TFTS tested various patterns of red and white or black and white stripes on the forward fuselage and wings to increase visibility. These tests were in vain, since F-15As were soon repainted in the Compass Ghost Gray scheme of overall Light Ghost Gray (FS36375), with portions of the upper surfaces in Dark Ghost Gray (FS36320). This camouflage scheme

Wingtip Development

YF-15

Straight Wingtip

F-15A

Raked Wingtip, with 4 Square Feet (0.4 M²) Removed from Prototype Wingtip

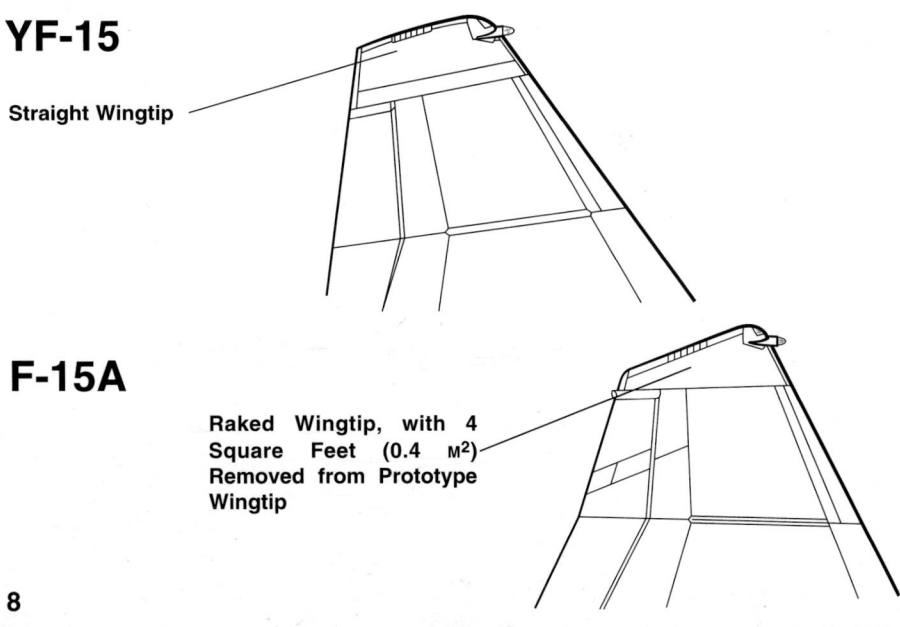

Elevon Development

YF-15

F-15A

Notch Cut Into Leading Edge

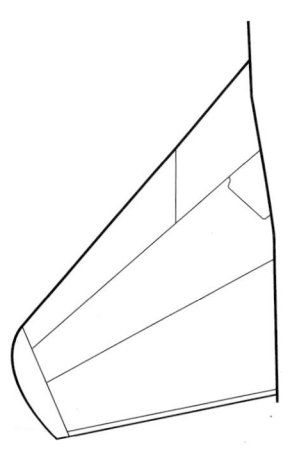
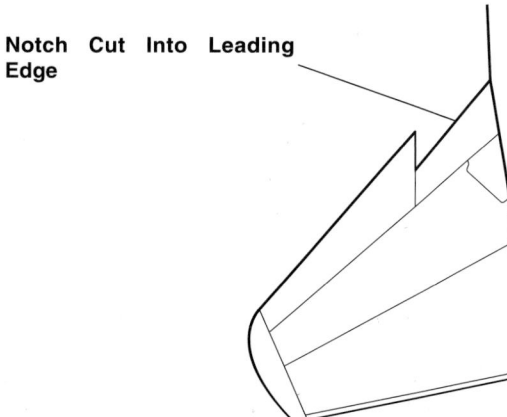

became the standard for all F-15As for over 15 years.

The USAF selected the 1st Tactical Fighter Wing (TFW) at Langley AFB, Virginia – just outside Norfolk, Virginia – to become the first operational F-15A wing. This unit consisted of the 27th Tactical Fighter Squadron (TFS), the 71st TFS, and the 94th TFS. The 1st TFW received its first F-15As in 1976, replacing F-4E Phantom IIs. Incidentally, the 1st TFW has been selected to become the first operational wing for the Lockheed Martin/Boeing F-22 Raptor. This aircraft is due to begin replacing the F-15 in USAF squadron service in 2005.

The Israel Defense Force/Air Force[1] (IDF/AF) was the first foreign air force to operate the F-15, receiving 23 F-15As from late 1976. Israeli F-15As have been credited with shooting down over 40 enemy aircraft, without loss to themselves.

In the 21st Century, F-15As operate with various Air National Guard (ANG) units across the United States. The 142nd Fighter Wing (FW) of the Oregon ANG is responsible for training ANG F-15 pilots at Kingsley Field in Portland. Other ANG F-15A units are the 125th FW (Florida ANG), 102nd FW (Massachusetts ANG), 131st FW (Missouri ANG), and the 159th FW (Louisiana ANG). ANG units are assigned to the USAF's Air Combat Command (ACC) and are responsible for air defense of the United States. Following the 11 September 2001 terrorist attacks on the World Trade Center in New York and the Pentagon in Washington, these Wings began flying Combat Air Patrols (CAPs) over most major American cities. This CAP program is designated Operation NOBLE EAGLE.

McDonnell Douglas built 361 F-15A Eagles at their St. Louis plant between 1972 and 1979, with 338 going to the USAF and 23 to Israel. This variant yielded to the similar appearing **F-15C Eagle** in 1979.

[1] In Hebrew, *Tsvah Haganah le Israel/Heyl Ha'Avir.*

NASA used the eighth F-15A (71-287, NASA 835) to test the dual-mode Highly Integrated Digital Electronic Control (HIDEC) program. The HIDEC control system allows an aircraft to land without using the flight controls, only using the throttle. This Eagle is painted overall glossy white with a flat black anti-glare panel. The small air brake is deployed and an air data probe is fitted to the nose. (NASA)

An F-15A (76-0119) lands at Nellis AFB, Nevada following a training mission. The larger speed brake deployed at a 45° angle, which caused less buffeting than the earlier small speed brake, which opened at a larger angle. This Eagle was assigned to the USAF Fighter Weapons School (FWS), 47th Fighter Weapons Wing (FWW) at Nellis, which trains USAF pilots in the best tactics for their aircraft. (Bob Binden)

All F-15s, including this 325th FW F-15A-14-MC (75-0055), are equipped with an arresting hook to 'trap' an aircraft that has lost its brakes or hydraulics. The hook is fitted between the afterburner sections of the two engines. Although the hook gives the impression of a navalized aircraft, the F-15 is not 'carrier qualified;' however, McDonnell Douglas offered an F-15 version to the US Navy to replace the Grumman F-14 Tomcat. (Al Adcock)

A Pratt & Whitney F100-PW-100 engine is mounted on a maintenance trailer before installation on an F-15A. Improved versions of this afterburning turbofan engine power later Eagles. Titanium engine nozzle actuator covers, nicknamed 'turkey feathers,' are fitted on this engine. These 'turkey feathers' were later removed from F-15 engines to reduce maintenance problems.

An Escapac IC-7 ejection seat is installed on this F-15A. This seat was installed on F-15A/B aircraft through Block 17, and on all Israeli F-15A through D aircraft. F-15A Block 18 and later Eagles received the improved ACES II ejection seat. Internal Countermeasures Sets (ICS) are installed in the equipment bay aft of the seat. (Centurion Enterprises)

The F-15A instrument panel grouped armament controls on the port side, with the Vertical Situation Display (VSD) for radar returns placed between these and the instrument shroud. The black panel on the upper center has controls for the communications and Identification Friend or Foe (IFF) equipment. Navigation instruments are placed on the panel's center, with engine and fuel controls to starboard. F-15 cockpits are primarily Dark Gull Gray (FS36231) and black. (Centurion Enterprises)

Ejection Seat Development

Escapac IC-7 (Early F-15A/Bs, all Israeli F-15s)

McDonnell Douglas ACES II (from late F-15A/Bs, except Israeli aircraft)

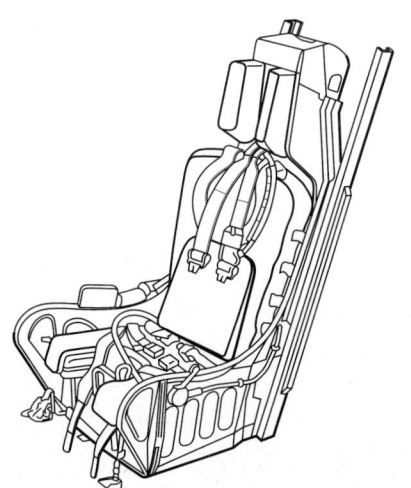

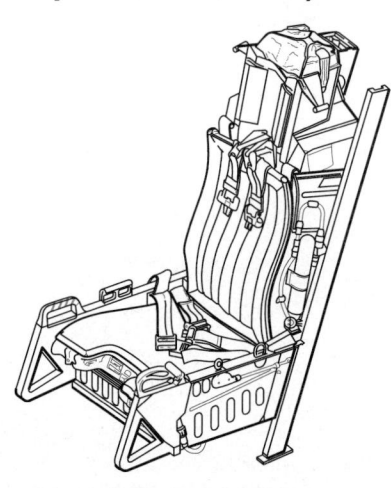

Munitions handlers approach the missile handling trailer to lift and carry the AIM-9 Sidewinder to a waiting 2nd FS F-15A (75-0022). The Squadron insignia appears on the port air intake, whose opening is covered by a tarpaulin. A 600 gallon fuel tank is mounted on the centerline stores pylon. This F-15A will soon be over the Gulf of Mexico stalking a QF-4E Phantom drone. (Al Adcock)

The AIM-9 Sidewinder missile is slid along the port outer stores pylon. Once locked in place, a red REMOVE BEFORE FLIGHT flag is pinned to the missile. A grounding cable is affixed to the stores pylon to prevent any accidental electrical sparking. The yellow cover over the seeker head will be removed before flight. (Al Adcock)

An F-15A-19-MC (77-0117) from the 8th Tactical Fighter Squadron (TFS), 49th Tactical Fighter Wing flies over the White Sands Missile Test Range, New Mexico in 1980. The Wing is based at nearby Holloman AFB. This Eagle is fully armed with four AIM-7 Sparrow and four AIM-9 Sidewinder missiles. The Squadron (now the 8th Fighter Squadron) currently flies the Lockheed F-117A Nighthawk 'stealth fighter.' (USAF)

A 48th Fighter Interceptor Squadron (FIS) F-15A-18-MC (76-0119) fires an AIM-7 Sparrow missile out over the Gulf of Mexico south of Tyndall AFB. The 48th FIS at Langley AFB, Virginia became the first operational F-15 Air Defense Tactical Air Command (ADTAC) squadron in August of 1981. Its aircraft had blue and white tail markings. (McDonnell Douglas)

Four F-15A-20-MCs from the 59th TFS, 33rd TFW at Eglin AFB fly along Florida's Gulf Coast in the late 1970s. The Block 20 aircraft were the last F-15As built by McDonnell-Douglas before production switched to the F-15C. The tail stripes are yellow and the Eagles are each fitted with a single 600 gallon centerline fuel tank. (McDonnell Douglas)

This F-15A-13-MC (75-0042) is marked as the 'flagship' (Squadron Commander's aircraft) of the 95th FS, 325th FW at Tyndall AFB. Two white stars are painted on the blue tail band, above the Air Combat Command (ACC) insignia. The Wing insignia is placed on the starboard intake side. Covers placed over the intake prevent 'FOD' (Foreign Object Damage) from entering the engine intakes. (Al Adcock)

Four F-15A-11-MCs (74-092 through 095) fly over snow covered mountains in Alaska. The Eagles are assigned to the 43rd TFS, 21st TFW at Elmendorf AFB, Alaska. All aircraft are armed with four AIM-7 Sparrow missiles along the fuselage sides and four AIM-9 Sidewinder missiles on the wing pylons. (McDonnell Douglas)

This F-15A-17-MC (76-0101) was assigned to the 3246th Test Wing at Eglin AFB. It carries a centerline mounted Westinghouse/Loral ALQ-131 (Deep) Electronic Countermeasures (ECM) pod during tests in the 1980s. The ECM pod is designed to jam radar signals and give false readings to enemy radar systems. The fin stripe is white with red 'shock' diamonds. (USAF)

This 6512th TS F-15A-17-MC (76-0084) from Edwards AFB was used to test and launch the Vought ASM-135A Anti-Satellite (ASAT) missile in the mid 1980s. The 17-foot (5.2 M) long, 2650 pound (1202 KG) ASAT missile successfully shot down the Solwind P78-1 satellite on 13 September 1985. The ASM-135A violated a US/Soviet treaty against ASAT weapons and no production was undertaken. (LTV)

Two F-15As from the 123rd FS 'Red Hawks,' 142nd FW/Operational Group fly high over the Oregon coast on a training mission. The nearest aircraft is F-15A-18-MC (77-0063) and the farthest is F-15A-13MC (75-0040) – the oldest operational F-15A in the US forces inventory. (USAF)

The last F-15A (76-0028) assigned to the 405th TTW at Luke AFB departs the active runway on 20 December 1991. The Eagle was en route to the 123rd FS, 142nd FG, Oregon ANG at Portland International Airport. The F-15 is fitted with a 'three pack' of 600 gallon extended range fuel tanks. The 405th TTW was the USAF's first F-15 Eagle unit. (USAF)

This F-15A-19-MC (77-0100) of the 101st FS, 102nd FW flies an Operation NOBLE EAGLE Combat Air Patrol (CAP) over New York City in late 2001. The Massachusetts ANG unit – based at Otis Air National Guard Base (ANGB) on Cape Cod – was one of the ANG units which patrolled US airspace following the terrorist attacks of 11 September 2001. (USAF)

F-15B (TF-15A) Eagle

The F-15B was originally designated the TF-15A, but this was changed when production began to differentiate between the single seat and the two seat models. The initial F-15B (71-290), a Block 3 aircraft, first flew on 7 July 1973. It was identical to the F-15A, with the exception of a second seat behind the pilot and a slightly larger canopy, which was bulged at the back to provide greater head room for the aft cockpit. The aircraft's overall weight increased by approximately 800 pounds (362.9 KG), to 27,300 pounds (12,383.3 KG) empty. The pilots sat in tandem in McDonnell Douglas Escapac IC-7 ejection seats; however, the IC-7 was soon replaced by the improved McDonnell Douglas ACES II[1] ejection seats. The ACES II equips all F-15s, except for those of Israel, which retain the earlier IC-7 seat. The F-15B front cockpit – usually occupied by the student pilot – retained the full flight controls and instruments of the F-15A. The aft cockpit has full flight controls, but reduced instruments.

The first operational two-seat Eagle was an F-15B-7-MC (73-108), which was the third production F-15B. The 555th Tactical Fighter Training Squadron (TFTS) officially accepted this F-15B, nicknamed TAC 1 (Tactical Air Command), at Luke AFB, Arizona on 14 November 1974. The 555th TFTS was assigned to the 58th Tactical Fighter Training Wing (TFTW) at Luke and operated as the F-15 Replacement Training Unit (RTU). TAC 1 was painted in the original Air Superiority Blue camouflage for F-15s. F-15Bs were soon repainted in the Compass Ghost Gray scheme standardized for air superiority Eagles.

In 1976, the second F-15B (71-291) was painted in Bicentennial red, white, and blue colors to commemorate the United States of America's 200th birthday. This Eagle made a world tour with stops at all major air shows and made some flights with the USAF Thunderbirds flight demonstration team. In 1980, 71-291 was used as the test bed for the Strike Eagle program, an anticipated replacement aircraft for the General Dynamics F-111. This F-15B was fitted with

[1]ACES: Advanced Concept Ejection Seat

The first F-15B (ex-TF-15A, 71-290) is painted overall white with dark blue (approximately FS15044) accents on the fuselage, wings, and tail surfaces. Golden rectangles on the wings have white oval access panels. The F-15 Eagle emblem is painted on the upper vertical stabilizer while the numeral 1 indicates the first F-15B. (Boeing)

This F-15B-7-MC (73-108) was the first operational Eagle and was named TAC 1 (for Tactical Air Command). It returned to Luke AFB, Arizona on 17 November 1991 – exactly 17 years after it ushered the Eagle into TAC service at Luke. The aircraft is painted in the original Air Superiority Blue finish of flat (FS35450) upper surfaces and glossy (FS15450) undersurfaces. This F-15B was used to introduce USAF pilots to the world's hottest jet fighter. (USAF)

F-15A Eagle

F-15B Eagle

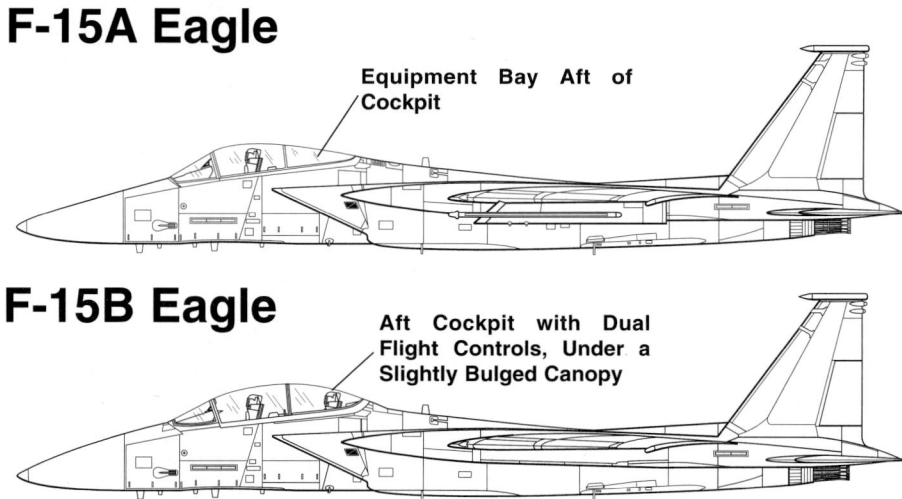

FAST Pack (Fuel And Sensor Tactical) Conformal Fuel Tanks (CFTs), FLIR/LANTIRN[2] targeting and navigation pods, and improved Hughes AN/APG-70 synthetic aperture radar. It was repainted in the European I wrap-around 'lizard' camouflage scheme of Dark Green (FS34092), Light Green (FS34102), and Gunship Gray (FS36081). All of the Strike Eagle tests were successful and the USAF ordered the F-15E into series production.

The first F-15B (71-290) was initially used for flight tests, until the USAF selected it for modification under the 'Agile Eagle' program. This became the Short Take-Off and Landing/Maneuvering Technology Demonstrator (STOL/MTD), a joint USAF/McDonnell Douglas program. The F-15B was modified with stabilators from a McDonnell Douglas F/A-18 Hornet, which were fitted to the upper air intake edges to serve as canard wings. A four channel fly-by-wire flight control was integrated with the propulsion controls and an AN/APG-70 radar system was installed. A strengthened undercarriage designed for unimproved landing strips was fitted. Following these modifications, the aircraft first flew on 7 September 1988. It was then redesignated **NF-15B**; the N prefix indicating that the airframe was not expected to be configured back to its original status.

While McDonnell Douglas was modifying the first F-15B for the STOL/MTD program, Pratt & Whitney developed a pair of two-dimensional thrust vectoring, thrust reversing engine nozzles. These replaced the standard circular dilating engine nozzles. The NF-15B had the new thrust-vectoring nozzles installed and made its first flight in this configuration on 19 May 1989. The tests demonstrated much reduced landing runs and take off rotation speeds reduced from 150 MPH (241.4 KMH) to only 42 MPH (67.6 KMH). This aircraft was painted in a colorful red, white, and blue scheme throughout its flight test program.

McDonnell Douglas built 58 F-15Bs, with 56 going to the USAF and the other two sold to the Israel Defense Force/Air Force (IDF/AF), which operates them with their F-15As. The F-15B presently serves with Air National Guard (ANG) units in the US in the primary role of training and introducing pilots to the F-15A Eagle.

[2]FLIR: Forward Looking Infra-Red; LANTIRN: Low-Altitude Navigation and Targeting, Infra-Red, for Night

NASA uses this F-15B-12-MC (74-141, NASA 836) as a test aircraft to constantly upgrade various F-15 systems and to carry out aerodynamic programs for other systems. This Eagle is painted in the standard NASA scheme of glossy white overall with a flat black anti-glare panel. Blue stripes are painted on the fuselage side and NASA is red on the vertical stabilizers. (NASA)

The F-15B-11-MC (74-139) in the foreground is painted in an experimental disruptive paint scheme designed by aviation artist Keith Ferris. This F-15B and two similarly painted F-15As, which are parked between aircraft 102 and 097, were assigned to the 405th TTW at Luke AFB during 1976. The Ferris scheme was not adopted after tests in the mid-1970s. The F-15B canopy's rear section was slightly raised to improve headroom for the second pilot. (USAF)

The second F-15B-4-MC (71-291) was painted with the American Revolution Bicentennial emblem on the vertical stabilizer in 1976. The nose, wing tips, and tail surfaces are progressively painted red, white, and blue. This aircraft is not fitted with the 20MM cannon in the starboard wing root, which was normally found on F-15Bs. The Eagle was flown on a world tour to demonstrate its capabilities and drum up sales to foreign countries. (USAF)

During the US Bicentennial celebration, several USAF aircraft were painted red, white, and blue to commemorate 200 years of freedom. The second F-15B appears at the 1976 Farnborough, England air show armed with inert AIM-7 Sparrow air-to-air missiles. Flags under the windshield show the countries this Eagle visited. (John Smith and Rob Braithwaite)

The second F-15B (71-291) fulfilled many roles during its long and illustrious career. This Block 4 aircraft served as the developmental aircraft for the F-15E 'Strike Eagle' program. It was also used to test the FAST Pack Conformal Fuel Tanks (CFTs) and LANTIRN targeting pods. This F-15B is painted in the wrap around European I 'lizard' camouflage scheme of Dark Green (FS34092), Light Green (FS34102), and Gunship Gray (FS36081). The aircraft is armed with Mk 7 dispensers for the Mk 20 Rockeye Cluster Bomb Units (CBUs) under the wings. AIM-9 Sidewinder Air-to-Air Missiles (AAMs) were fitted on the wing pylon sides. (via David Sconyers)

A F-15B-17-MC (76-0140) from the 445th Flight Test Squadron (FTS) at Edwards AFB appears at Canadian Forces Base (CFB) Cold Lake, Alberta, Canada in 1999. The aircraft is painted overall white with black anti-glare panel and Insignia Red (FS11136) vertical stabilizers. The tail band above the Air Force Material Command (AFMC) insignia is black and white. (Chris Smallenberg)

This F-15B-19-MC (77-0161) is assigned to the 3246th Test Wing (TW) at Eglin AFB, Florida. The Wing flies a mix of various aircraft to test and evaluate current and future weapons for the USAF. This Eagle appears to be armed with 500 pound (226.8 KG) Mk 82 bombs painted black and white for photographic purposes. Red shock diamonds are painted on the white tail band. (USAF)

The commander of the 1st Air Force, Major General Paul Brown, flew this F-15B-13-MC (75-0082) from Tyndall AFB, Florida in 1992. The crew access ladder is in place and the air intake covers have two stars indicating the commander's flag rank. The nose art depicts an eagle emblazoned over a sun with the name BAY COUNTY, where Tyndall AFB is located. (Al Adcock)

The F-15B aft instrument panel has fewer instruments and controls than the front instrument panel, which is identical to those on single-seat F-15As. Instructor pilots usually occupy the rear seat on two-seat Eagles, with the student in front. Communications controls are mounted beside the VSD, with flight instruments below. Engine and fuel indicators are placed on the starboard panel section. (Detail & Scale Photo by Bert Kinzey)

The NF-15B-3-MC Short Takeoff and Landing Maneuver Technology Demonstrator (STOL/MTD) (71-290) is parked on McDonnell Douglas' St. Louis ramp in May of 1989. The Air Force Systems Command (AFSC) insignia is painted on the upper vertical stabilizer, above the STOL/MTD program insignia. It is fitted with Pratt & Whitney thrust reversing and vectoring engine exhausts. These nozzles were unavailable when the NF-15B made its first flight on 7 September 1988. (McDonnell Douglas)

The NF-15B STOL/MTD first flew with the thrust vectoring nozzles on 10 May 1989. Horizontal stabilizers from a McDonnell Douglas F/A-18 Hornet were mounted on this aircraft's engine inlets. These stabilizers served as canards to increase maneuverability. A test instrumentation boom mounted on the F-15B's nose recorded flight data for the test pilot and for engineers on the ground. (McDonnell Douglas)

The F-15B STOL/MTD (71-290) arrives at Edwards AFB, California from St. Louis on 16 June 1989. It was flown by Major Bud Jenschke from the Air Force Flight Test Center and Larry Walker of McDonnell Douglas. A 600 gallon (2271.2 L) fuel tank is mounted on the centerline for this ferry flight. This aircraft was painted overall glossy white, with red and blue trim. After arrival at Edwards, the F-15B STOL/MTD performed additional tests for the USAF's 'Agile Eagle' program. (McDonnell Douglas)

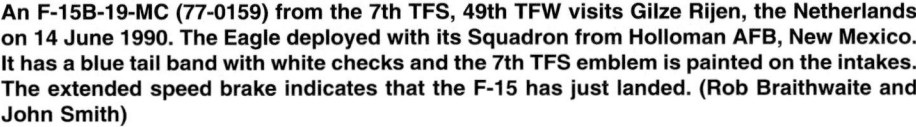

An F-15B-19-MC (77-0159) from the 7th TFS, 49th TFW visits Gilze Rijen, the Netherlands on 14 June 1990. The Eagle deployed with its Squadron from Holloman AFB, New Mexico. It has a blue tail band with white checks and the 7th TFS emblem is painted on the intakes. The extended speed brake indicates that the F-15 has just landed. (Rob Braithwaite and John Smith)

The 142nd FW, Oregon ANG flies this F-15B-14-MC (75-0086) from Portland International Airport. A detachment operates from Kingsley Field near Klamath Falls, Oregon. This Wing trains ANG pilots and provides air defense of the US West Coast. The 142nd FW is one of the few USAF units that does not use tail codes, opting instead for a subdued eagle emblem. All F-15 Eagles have unpainted aft lower fuselage surfaces. (USAF)

This F-15B-15-MC (76-0125) is assigned to the 125th FW 'Jaguars,' Florida Air National Guard (ANG) from Jacksonville International Airport. The Eagle is used in support of the 1st Air Force, which directs ANG units responsible for air defense of the United States. The Jaguar emblem on the vertical stabilizers is also the insignia for the National Football League's Jacksonville Jaguars. (Via Captain Richard Bittner, 125th Fighter Wing)

This F-15B-13-MC (75-0082) was assigned to the Commander of the 1st Air Force at Tyndall AFB, Florida in 1992. The red (top), yellow, and blue tail stripes of the Tyndall-based 325th FW are painted on the vertical stabilizers, above the Air Combat Command (ACC) insignia. The emblems of the 1st AF (front) and the 325th FW are painted on the intake side. (Al Adcock)

The first F-15C Eagle (78-0468) was a Block 21 airframe, which was tested at Edwards AFB, California in 1978. The aircraft is fitted with FAST (Fuel And Sensor Tactical) Pack Conformal Fuel Tanks (CFTs) that each hold an additional 4400 pounds (1995.8 KG) of fuel. The C model was also fitted with LANTIRN targeting/radar pods and a single 600 gallon (2271.2 L) external fuel tank. (USAF)

The F-15C prototype was equipped with a nose-mounted air data test probe for tests at Edwards AFB. Three 600 gallon fuel tanks are mounted on the centerline and wing pylons. AIM-9 Sidewinder missiles are fitted to the wing pylons, while 500 pound (226.8 KG) Mk 82 bombs are mounted on the FAST Packs. Black and white photo reference markings are painted on the fuselage. (USAF)

F-15C Eagle

The F-15C represented an improvement over the F-15A, although there were no visual external differences between the two variants. The first F-15C (78-0468) was a Block 21 airframe and it first flew on 26 February 1979. The aircraft was tested at McDonnell Douglas in St. Louis before it was flown to Edwards AFB, where USAF flight-testing soon began over the California desert.

The F-15C prototype was flown with the FAST (Fuel And Sensor Tactical) Pack Conformal Fuel Tanks (CFTs), which incorporated weapons pylons. A prototype Martin Marietta LANTIRN (Low Altitude Navigation and Targeting, Infra-Red, for Night) pod was also installed. The CFTs come in a few different versions that incorporated the carriage of fuel and sensor packages in various configurations. One version carries only fuel and no sensor packages, while others contain sensor and avionics packages and up to six weapons pylons. CFTs are usually carried for extended range missions in place of carrying the three 600 gallon (2271.2 L) fuel tanks. Mission requirements vary and for maximum endurance ranges three 600 gallon fuel tanks as well as the conformal tanks will yield an unrefueled range of over 3500 miles (5632.6 KM). One of the improvements made to the F-15C is in increased internal fuel capacity. Tanks added to the wing leading edges, trailing edges, and fuselage combine to increase internal fuel from 1850 gallons (7003 L) in the F-15A to 2070 gallons (7835.8 L) in the F-15C.

The changes made to the F-15C airframe increased its empty weight from the F-15A's 27,000 pounds (12,247.2 KG) to 28,600 pounds (12,973 KG). The F-15C's landing gear, wheels, and tires were strengthened to compensate for this increased weight. The F-15C was now rated for a maximum take off weight of 68,000 pounds (30,844.8 KG) with conformal fuel tanks, three 600 gallon (2271.2 L) external fuel tanks, four AIM-7 Sparrow AAMs, and four AIM-9 Sidewinder AAMs. To insure the airframe's integrity, an overload warning system is fitted to allow the pilot to safely maneuver through nine Gs of the entire flight envelope, a certain testament to the strength of the airframe. The F-15C's dimensions remain the same as for the earlier F-15A. This variant has a wingspan of 42 feet 9 3/4 inches (13 M), a length of 63 feet 9 inches (19.4 M), and a height of 18 feet 5 1/2 inches (5.6 M).

The F-15C avionics and radar suite was improved with installation of the Hughes AN/APG-70 synthetic aperture radar to replace the firm's earlier AN/APG-63. The AN/APG-70 is being installed during various Multi Stage Improvement Programs (MSIPs) designed to extend the airframe and avionics life of earlier F-15s. This newer radar has a 1000 kilobyte memory and it also incorporates high-speed signal processors for data storage and retrieval. It is used to track targets for both the missiles and 20MM M61A1 Vulcan cannon. The AN/APG-70 demonstrates an improved rate of reliability over the earlier AN/APG-63 set.

The F-15C can be configured for either the air-to-air role or the air-to-ground role. In the air-to-air role up to four AIM-7 Sparrow or AIM-120 AMRAAM and four AIM-9 Sidewinder missiles can be carried, with or without CFTs. For the air-to-ground missions, the CFTs are fitted with weapons pylons to carry up to eighteen 500 pound (226.8 KG) bombs on Multiple Ejector Racks (MERs). CFTs are infrequently fitted to F-15Cs, since they induce unwanted aerodynamic drag on the airframe. Mission commanders usually opt for the 600 gallon external tanks, since they can be jettisoned in flight before a fight while the CFTs cannot.

This model was originally powered by two Pratt & Whitney F-100-PW-100 turbofan engines, each delivering 23,830 pounds of afterburning thrust. Beginning in 1985, these engines were replaced by the improved, but lower power F-100-PW-220 turbofan engine. The -220 engine's greater reliability has greatly reduced the air stagnation problem that affected the -100 engine when full military power was applied. (Full military power is the maximum non-afterburning power setting.) The newer powerplant has increased airflow fans and a digital electronic engine control system to more closely monitor fuel and airflow. The F-100-PW-220 delivers a reduced rating of 23,450 pounds of afterburning thrust. It also demonstrated improved fuel economy to help extend the F-15C's range. A further refinement is the new Pratt & Whitney F-100-PW-229 turbofan engine, which produces 29,000 pounds of afterburning thrust. This powerplant is being retrofitted to F-15Cs as it becomes available.

The Pacific Air Forces' 18th Tactical Fighter Wing (TFW) (now the 18th Wing) at Kadena Air Base (AB), Okinawa began receiving the first F-15Cs from July of 1979. Not only was it the first Eagle unit in the Pacific, but it was also one of the first F-15 outfits to adopt the darker Mod Eagle scheme on their aircraft. This color scheme – overall Light Gray (FS36251), with Dark Gray (FS37176) upper surface portions – replaced the earlier Compass Ghost Gray scheme on US air superiority F-15s from the early 1990s.

The 32nd Tactical Fighter Squadron (TFS) 'Wolfhounds,' based at Soesterberg AB, the Netherlands, was the next unit to receive the new F-15C in June of 1980. The F-15C was soon assigned to the 54th TFS, 21st TFW at Elmendorf AFB, Alaska and the 57th Fighter Interceptor Squadron (FIS) at Keflavik Naval Station, Iceland. The 57th usually carried CFTs and a single 600 gallon centerline fuel tank on their Combat Air Patrols (CAPs) on intercept missions out of Keflavik. F-15Cs also replaced F-15As assigned to the 1st TFW (Langley AFB, Virginia) and the 36th TFW (Bitburg AB, West Germany).

In 1981, the Royal Saudi Air Force[2] (RSAF) began receiving the first of 46 F-15C Eagles ordered under a Foreign Military Sales (FMS) program called Peace Sun. The F-15Cs equipped three RSAF squadrons: Number 5 at King Fahd AB, Taif; No 6 at King Khalid AB, Khamis Mushait; and No 13 at King Abdul Aziz AB, Dhahran. The F-15Cs are camouflaged in the Compass Ghost Gray scheme with green English and Arabic markings. Under FMS program Peace Sun III, the Israel Defense Force/Air Force began receiving Block 27 F-15Cs for their 106 Squadron at Tel Nov.

On 2 August 1990, the Iraqi forces of Saddam Hussein attacked Kuwait, their neighbor to the south. The first USAF F-15C units to respond were the 27th TFS and 71st TFS, both of the 1st TFW at Langley AFB, Virginia. They were soon to be joined by the 58th TFS/33rd FW, Eglin AFB, Florida, the 53rd and 525th TFS/36th TFW, Bitburg AB, Germany, and the 32nd TFS/32nd Tactical Fighter Group, Soesterberg AB. When Operation DESERT STORM began on 17 January 1991, the F-15C Tactical Fighter Squadrons made quick work of Iraqi Air Force elements that dared to meet them in air-to-air combat. When the dust finally settled on 25 January – a mere nine days later – USAF F-15Cs shot down 36 Iraqi Air Force aircraft. Pilots of the 58th TFS claimed 17 of those kills, prompting them to erect a sign at Wing headquarters reading 'World's Largest Distributor of MiG Parts.' AIM-7 Sparrows were responsible for 25 of the 36 Iraqi aircraft downed by USAF F-15Cs during DESERT STORM. Two other Iraqi aircraft were downed by a Saudi F-15C on 24 January.

In 1992, the 325th Fighter Wing (FW) of the Air Education and Training Command (AETC) at Tyndall AFB, Florida began converting from the F-15A to the F-15C. The F-15As were reassigned to Air National Guard squadrons. This change insured that the student pilots would be flying the Eagle variant they would fly once they rotated to the operational squadron level.

McDonnell Douglas built 472 F-15Cs from 1979 until 1992. These included 408 for the USAF, 18 for Israel, and 46 for Saudi Arabia. The F-15C Eagle will continue in USAF front line squadron service until it is replaced by the Lockheed Martin/Boeing F-22 Raptor some time in 2005, depending on production rates authorized by the US Congress.

[2]In Arabic, *Al Quwwat al Jawwiya al Aalakiya as Sa'udiya*.

The 4485th TS borrowed F-15C-38-MC (84-0018) from the 59th TFS to test the new AIM-120 AMRAAM air-to-air missile. Cameras for recording missile launches are mounted on orange outer wing fairings. An Air Combat Maneuvering Instrumentation (ACMI) pod is fitted to the Number 8 station on the starboard wing pylon. Data from the ACMI pod evaluates the F-15's performance while firing the AMRAAMs. (USAF)

Five F-15Cs of the 18th Tactical Fighter Wing (now 18th Wing) fly over Diamond Head on the Hawaiian Island of Oahu. The Eagles were on their way to their home of Kadena AB, Okinawa. The 18th TFW was the first operational F-15C unit. The near Eagle (78-0492) has extended its speed brake the full 45°. (McDonnell Douglas)

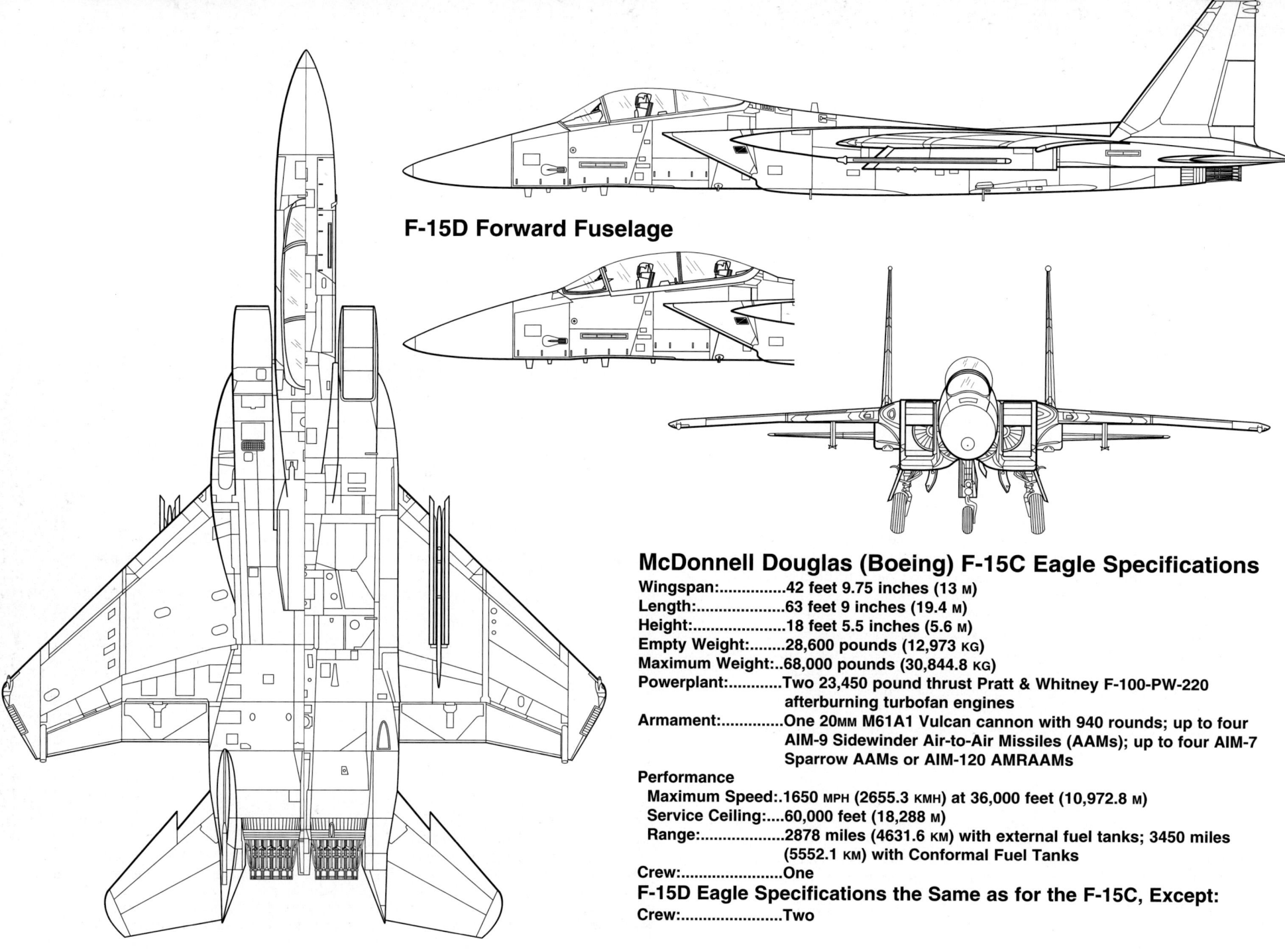

The F-15C nose landing gear consists of a single main strut and wheel. The gear retracts forward into the fuselage. Taxi (upper) and landing (lower) lights are mounted on the strut for use at night and in bad weather conditions. F-15 landing gears, wells, and door inner surfaces are Glossy White (FS17875) to aid in detecting hydraulic leaks. (Lou Drendel)

The F-15C main landing gear is identical to that for the F-15A/B, but strengthened to support higher aircraft weights. Each gear has a single wheel, whose cooling holes allowed air to pass to the anti-skid brakes. Eagle main wheels were painted Glossy Black (FS17038) until they were repainted Glossy White in the early 1990s for increased leak and wheel crack detection. The main gear retracts aft to lie horizontally within the fuselage.

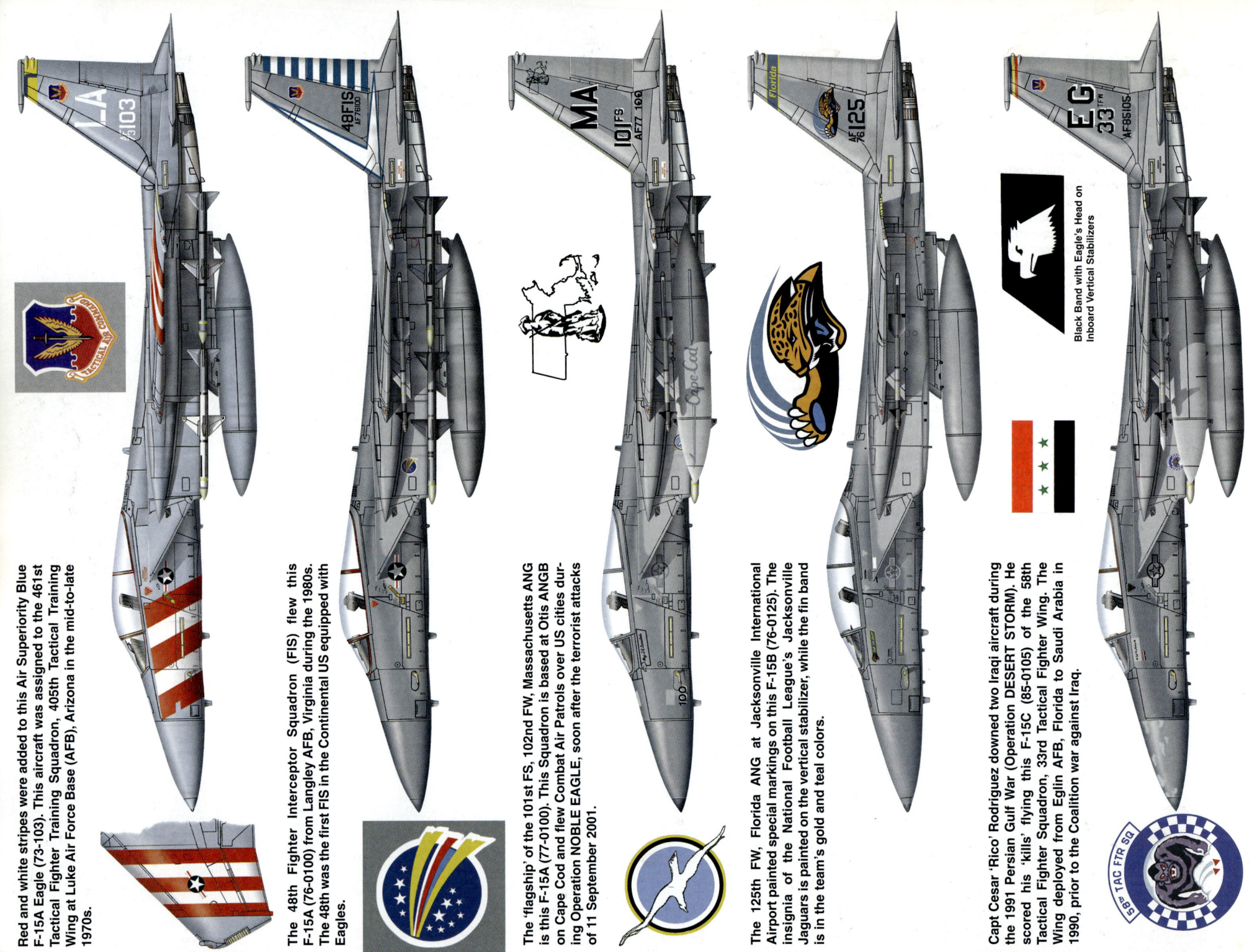

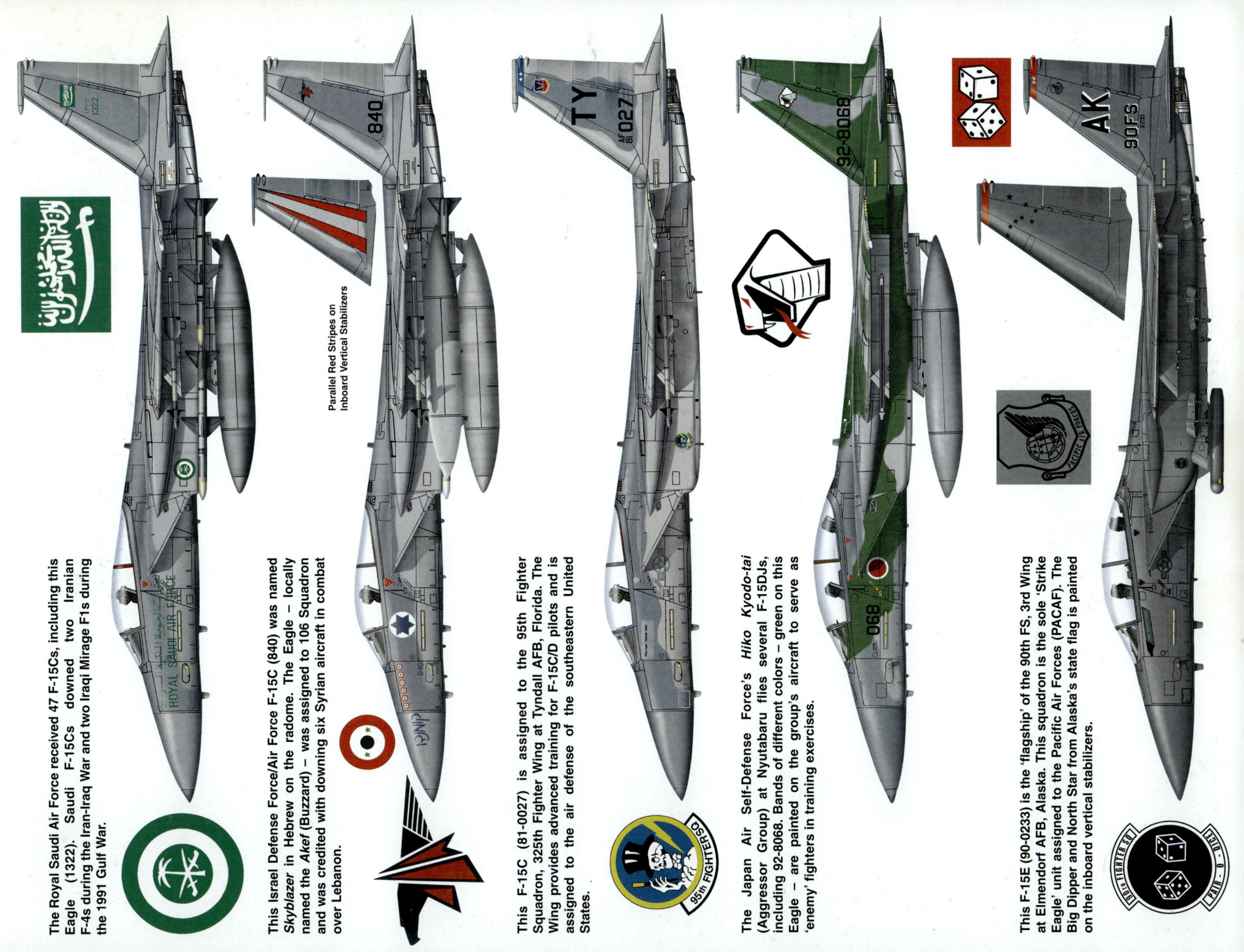

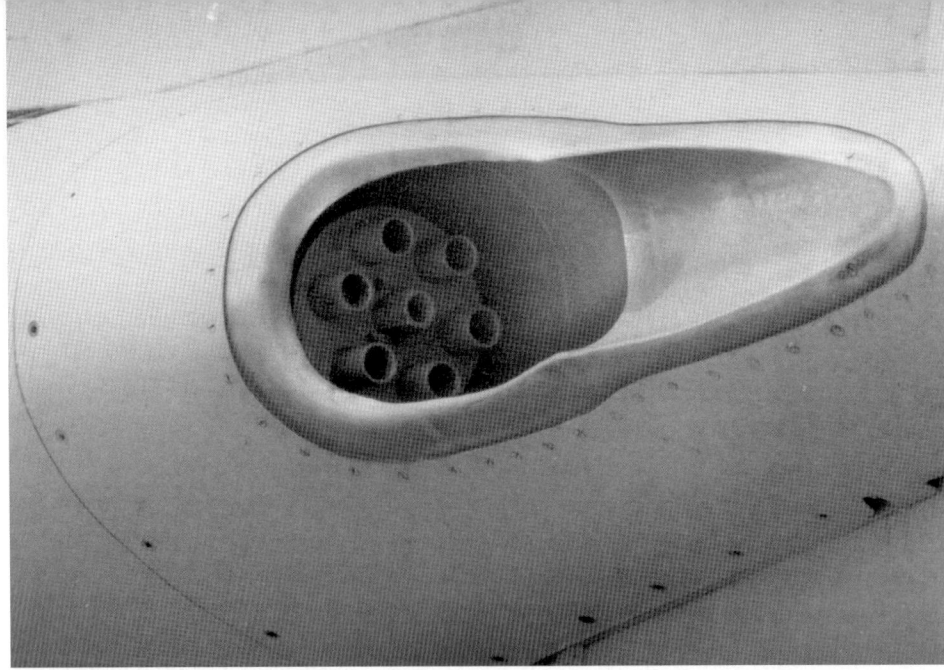

The 20MM General Electric M61A1 Vulcan cannon is mounted in the starboard wing root of all F-15 Eagle models, including this F-15C. The six-barrel rotary cannon has a firing rate of up to 6000 rounds per minute. F-15Cs are supplied with 940 rounds of ammunition for this weapon, which is used for close-in air and ground attacks. (Al Adcock)

This 325th FW F-15C is armed with two AIM-9 Sidewinder Air-to-Air Missiles (AAMs) on the wing pylon. These heat-seeking AAMs are mounted on rails fitted to the pylon's sides. Protective covers are placed over the AIM-9's sensitive seeker heads. An AIM-7 Sparrow Semi-Active Radar Homing (SARH) AAM is fitted to the port forward fuselage station. (Al Adcock)

A 33rd TFW F-15C-39-MC (85-0102) comes into position under a tanker to 'top off' its fuel tanks during a Combat Air Patrol (CAP) mission over Iraq in 1991. The aircraft is armed with two AIM-9 Sidewinders, four AIM-7 Sparrows, and two AIM-120 AMRAAMs. Captain Anthony Murphy shot down three Iraqi fighters – a MiG-23 (Flogger) and two Su-22s (Fitters) – with Sparrow missiles while flying this Eagle on 7 February 1991. (USAF)

This F-15C-38-MC (AD, 84-0018) flies on a test mission from Eglin AFB. The aircraft is assigned to the 3246th Test Squadron, whose white tail band has red shock diamonds. Two AIM-120 AMRAAM missiles are carried on the port fuselage CFTs, while orange fairings for cameras are mounted on the starboard CFTs. These cameras recorded the missiles' release from the aircraft. (USAF)

An F-15C-36-MC (OT, 83-0039) flies over the Highway 98 bridge leading to Destin, Florida. The Eagle is assigned to the 4485th Test Squadron (TS), 3246th Test Wing of the Tactical Air Warfare Center (TAWC) at nearby Eglin AFB. The tail band has black, white, and red checks, while *Tactical Air Warfare Center* is painted at the base of the vertical stabilizer. (USAF)

An F-15C banks away from the camera aircraft to reveal the FAST Pack Conformal Fuel Tanks (CFTs) and four practice AIM-9 Sidewinder missiles on the wing pylons. Low-visibility insignia on air superiority F-15s replaced the full color national insignia in the 1980s. The 'turkey feathers' that once covered the engine afterburners' actuators are removed. (USAF)

The 1st TFW deployed 48 F-15C Eagles from Langley AFB, Virginia for Operation DESERT SHIELD. This Operation defended Saudi Arabia and the Middle East from Iraqi invasion from August of 1990 until January of 1991. A 27th FS Eagle prepares to fly a CAP from Dhahran AB, Saudi Arabia armed with AIM-9 Sidewinder and AIM-120 AMRAAM air-to-air missiles. (USAF)

This 59th FS, 33rd FW F-15C-41-MC (86-0154) undergoes routine maintenance in a hangar at Eglin AFB. The 33rd FW insignia is placed on the starboard intake, while the 20MM cannon fairing in the wing root has been removed. Both the speed brake and the tail hook are extended. An eagle's head appears on a black inboard stabilizer band. (Al Adcock)

This F-15C-41-MC (86-0162) is prepared for a Dissimilar Air Combat Training (DACT) mission from Eglin AFB, Florida in 1992. The Eagle is assigned to the 390th FS 'Wild Boars,' 366th Operational Group (OG) from Mountain Home AFB, Idaho. The Squadron honed its air-to-air skills through DACT at Eglin. The F-15C displays only the MO tail code and serial number on the vertical stabilizer. Three 600 gallon external fuel tanks are fitted to this Eagle. (Al Adcock)

Maintainers change the starboard Pratt & Whitney F-100-PW-200 engine of the 33rd TFW's 'flagship' F-15C-39-MC (85-0103). This change occurred at King Faisal AB, Tabuk, Saudi Arabia during Operation DESERT STORM. The F-15's engine can be changed within 30 minutes. The outboard tail band of (from top) blue, yellow, and red represents the 33rd TFW's three squadrons. (USAF)

Maintenance crews fit a 600 gallon external fuel tank to the starboard wing pylon of an F-15C–27-MC (80-0006) in early 1991. The Eagle was assigned to the 36th Tactical Fighter Wing (TFW), which deployed from its home of Bitburg AB, Germany to Incirlik AB, Turkey for Operation DESERT STORM. F-15Cs patrolled northern Iraq during and after the Persian Gulf War. The tail band is (from front) red, yellow, and blue. (USAF)

The F-15C 'flagship' of the 27th TFS, 1st TFW flies over the Great Pyramids of Giza, Egypt. This Eagle is joined by two Egyptian Air Force aircraft, an F-4E Phantom II (middle) and a Dassault Mirage III. The 27th TFS was in Egypt for BRIGHT STAR, a joint US and Egyptian military exercise.

Two 1st TFW F-15Cs are parked outside Hardened Aircraft Shelters (HASs) at Dhahran AB, Saudi Arabia during Operation DESERT SHIELD. Three 600 gallon external fuel tanks, AIM-9 Sidewinders, and AIM-7 Sparrows are mounted on these Eagles. The 1st TFW deployed the first Eagles to Saudi Arabia in August of 1990 to keep the Iraqi Air Force at bay. (USAF)

An F-15C receives fuel from a KC-135 tanker aircraft. The boom is 'flown' into the receptacle by the tanker's boom operator, using two controllable vanes on the boom's end. In-flight refueling greatly extends the F-15C's range to where it is limited only by the pilot's endurance. (USAF)

This F-15C-34-MC (82-0037) flies a Combat Air Patrol (CAP) over Iraq during DESERT STORM. The Eagle was assigned to the 27th TFS, 1st TFW. The F-15C is fully armed with AIM-7 and AIM-9 AAMs, and is fitted with three 600 gallon fuel tanks under the wings and on the centerline. Capt Steve Tate of the Wing's 71st TFS scored the first 'kill' of the war on 17 January 1991, when he downed an Iraqi Mirage F1.

Two 36th TFW F-15C fly a Combat Air Patrol (CAP) over northern Iraq during the 1991 Persian Gulf War. Both Eagles are armed with AIM-7 Sparrows and AIM-9 Sidewinders and carry three 600 gallon (2271.2 L) external fuel tanks. The near aircraft is F-15C-38-MC (84-0027) of the Wing's 53rd TFS. Captain Benjamin Powell flew this Eagle when he shot down an Iraqi MiG-23 and a Mirage F1EQ with AIM-7s on 27 January 1991. (USAF)

Captain Cesar 'Rico' Rodriguez Jr. from the 58th TFS 'Gorillas,' 33rd TFW flew this F-15C-40-MC (85-0114) during part of Operation DESERT STORM in 1991. He shot down two Iraqi aircraft, a MiG-23 (Flogger) and a MiG-29 (Fulcrum), while flying this Eagle. Two green stars on the nose represent those 'kills' on this Eagle at its home of Eglin AFB, Florida in 1992. (Al Adcock)

Captain Robert E. Graeter from the 58th TFS, 33rd TFW flew this F-15C (85-0105) during Operation DESERT STORM. He shot down two Iraqi Mirage F1 fighters using AIM-7 Sparrow missiles on 17 January 1991 – the first night of the Gulf War. Two green stars on the fuselage under the windshield represent Graeter's kills. (Al Adcock)

Captain John Kelk of the 58th TFS, 33rd TFW flew this F-15C-40-MC (85-0125) during Operation DESERT STORM. On 17 January 1991, he shot down an Iraqi MiG-21 (Fishbed) using an AIM-7 Sparrow missile. This Eagle was the 58th TFS 'flagship' and displayed a blue tail band and the 33rd TFW insignia on the air intake. (Al Adcock)

The commander of the 33rd Operational Group (OG), 33rd TFW flew this F-15C-42-MC (86-0178) during Operation DESERT STORM in 1991. The name GULF SPIRIT is superimposed over the map of Florida. The Wing's home of Eglin AFB is located in the Florida panhandle, on the Gulf of Mexico. Insignia of the Wing's 58th, 59th, and 60th TFSs appear on the engine intake sides. This Wing deployed to King Faisal AB, Tabuk, Saudi Arabia for the Gulf War. (Al Adcock)

Captain Rhory Draeger of the 58th TFS, 33rd TFW flew this F-15C-40-MC (85-0108) when he shot down an Iraqi MiG-23 on 17 January 1991 – the first night of Operation DESERT STORM. He fired an AIM-7 Sparrow that destroyed the Iraqi fighter. This Eagle displays the 9th Air Force and 33rd TFW insignias on the air intake and the GULF SPIRIT insignia on the nose. (Al Adcock)

In 1992, the 33rd FW at Eglin AFB began repainting their F-15Cs in the new 'Mod Eagle' camouflage of Dark Gray (FS37176) and Light Gray (FS36251). Markings are Light Gray on the Dark Gray surfaces. This F-15C-42-MC (86-0167) is assigned to the Wing's 60th FS. The vertical stabilizer displays the ACC insignia below the blue squadron tail band. (Al Adcock)

The 19th Fighter Squadron (FS) commander's F-15C lands at Elmendorf AFB, Alaska. This Squadron is assigned to the Elmendorf-based 3rd Wing (Wg). It is customary to paint the squadron designator on one aircraft, usually the squadron commander's aircraft, and call it the unit's 'flagship.' This F-15C has a blue tail stripe and no serial number is painted on the vertical stabilizer. (USAF)

A 493rd FS F-15C-35-MC (83-0015) launches from Aviano AB, Italy to support US forces in Bosnia-Herzegovina. This Eagle is camouflaged in the 'Mod Eagle' camouflage scheme, which was introduced in 1992. Three 600 gallon external fuel tanks increase the F-15C's operational range and time over target. (USAF)

Two F-15Cs assigned to the 18th Operational Group (OG), 5th Air Force fly over Kadena AB, Okinawa, Japan. The nearest F-15C (78-0477) is the 5th AF's 'flagship,' while flying lead is F-15C-21-MC (78-0480) from the 67th FS 'Fighting Cocks.' Both aircraft are in the 'Mod Eagle' camouflage pioneered by Pacific Air Forces (PACAF) F-15 squadrons. (USAF)

The 1st FW's 'flagship' F-15C Eagle flies near its home of Langley AFB, Virginia. The aircraft was just repainted in the darker 'Mod Eagle' finish now used by USAF air superiority F-15s. The FF tail code stands for First Fighter. The tail band is (from front) red, yellow, and blue to represent the 71st, 27th, and 94th Fighter Squadrons, respectively. (USAF)

Two 366th Wing (Wg) F-15Cs fly over the rugged Idaho countryside on a training mission from Mountain Home AFB, Idaho. The near aircraft is the 'flagship' of the 390th FS 'Wild Boars,' while the lead Eagle is the Wing's flagship.' Both aircraft are armed with Sparrow and Sidewinder Air-to-Air Missiles (AAMs). The 366th Wg is the USAF's 'air intervention' wing for rapid deployment to international hot spots – most recently over Afghanistan during Operation ENDURING FREEDOM. (USAF)

An F-15D-39-MC (85-0130) from the 58th FS, 33rd FW taxis to the active runway at Eglin AFB, Florida in July of 1992. The tail band is blue and the Squadron's badge is painted on the air intake. This Eagle is fitted with a 600 gallon centerline fuel tank and one AIM-9 Sidewinder missile on the port wing pylon. (Al Adcock)

The last F-15D built was this F-15D-41-MC (86-0182), assigned to the 59th FS, 33rd FW. This Eagle is being readied for flight from Eglin and will be flown solo with no 'back seater.' The aircraft is armed with an AIM-9 Sidewinder on the number eight (inner port) wing pylon station. (Al Adcock)

F-15D Eagle

The **F-15D Eagle** was basically a two seat F-15C, retaining all its dimensions, armament, and specifications. The first F-15D utilized the F-15C Block 21 airframe, which was modified to add a second seat behind the pilot, like in the earlier F-15B. Adding the second seat increased the F-15D's empty weight from the F-15C's 28,600 pounds (12,973 KG) to 29,400 pounds (13,335.8 KG). The maximum takeoff weight was restricted to 68,000 pounds (30,844.8 KG). This weight included the installation of 728 gallon (2755.8 L) Conformal Fuel Tanks (CFTs), three 600 gallon (2271.2 L) external fuel tanks, and either four AIM-7 Sparrow or AIM-120 AMRAAM Air-to-Air Missiles (AAMs) and four AIM-9 Sidewinder AAMs.

The first F-15D-21-MC (78-0561) made its maiden flight on 19 June 1979, some four months after the initial F-15C's first fight. The F-15D is essentially used as a trainer aircraft and to familiarize incoming pilots with squadron operations and procedures. It became operational alongside F-15Cs of the 1st Tactical Fighter Wing (TFW), Langley AFB, Virginia in December of 1981. This Wing (redesignated the 1st Fighter Wing in 1992) previously flew F-15A/B Eagles.

The 1st TFW became one of the first units deployed to Saudi Arabia in support of Operation DESERT SHIELD in 1990. Six F-15Ds assigned to the Wing's 27th and 71st Tactical Fighter Squadrons (TFSs) flew with the F-15Cs from Langley to Saudi bases. The F-15Ds flew fully armed Combat Air Patrols (CAPs) over Saudi Arabian airspace to guard against incursions by marauding Iraqi Air Force aircraft. They did not score any aerial victories during the ensuing Operation DESERT STORM, but they assisted in the Coalition effort to free Kuwait.

The name GLAMOROUS GLENNIS was painted in orange on the nose of an F-15D (84-0046) in 1997. This commemorated the breaking of the sound barrier by Captain Chuck Yeager in the Bell X-1 GLAMOROUS GLENNIS (46-062) on 17 October 1947. The X-1 was an experimental rocket powered aircraft designed solely to investigate transonic (faster than the speed of sound) flight. The commemorative flight occurred at Edwards AFB, California with then-Brigadier General Yeager at the controls. (The 1947 flight also took place at Edwards, then called Muroc Dry Lake.) This F-15D of the 415th Flight Test Squadron, 412th Test Wing was fitted with CFTs for the 1997 flight.

Three foreign air forces have chosen the F-15D for squadron service. The Israel Defense Force/Air Force (IDF/AF) received eight F-15Ds under Peace Fox III. It is highly probably that at least a few have scored aerial victories over their foes, but the IDF/AF has always been highly secretive about victories scored by their pilots. Sixteen F-15Ds were delivered to the Royal Saudi Air Force (RSAF) for its No 6, 13, and 42 Squadrons.

The Japan Air Self-Defense Force[1] (JASDF) received 28 aircraft designated the **F-15DJ**. McDonnell Douglas built the first 12 F-15DJs in St. Louis, while Mitsubishi Heavy Industries at Nagoya, Japan built the 16 remaining aircraft. The JASDF uses the F-15DJ for conversion training in front line squadrons and with the *Hiko Kyodo-tai* (Aggressor Group) based at Nyutabaru. The latter unit flies specially painted F-15DJs to serve as 'enemy' aircraft during air combat training exercises.

McDonnell Douglas built 134 F-15Ds, including 98 aircraft for USAF operational squadrons and flight test units. The remaining 36 aircraft were delivered to Israel (eight), Saudi Arabia (16), and Japan (12).

[1] In Japanese, *Nihon Koku Jieitai*.

An F-15D-34-MC (82-0046) from the 21st TFS, 1st TFW sits in a revetment at Dhahran, Saudi Arabia in November of 1990. The Squadron deployed from Langley AFB, Virginia for Operation DESERT SHIELD. The aircraft is fitted with AIM-9 Sidewinders and 600 gallon external fuel tanks. MIM-109 Patriot Surface-to-Air Missiles (SAMs) in the background protected the airfield from Iraqi Scud missile attacks. (McDonnell Douglas)

An F-15D-29-MC (80-0058) assigned to the 54th FS, 3rd Wing is parked at Elmendorf AFB, Alaska. The Alaska state flag – a dark blue field with yellow stars forming the constellation Ursa Major ('Big Dipper') and Polaris the North Star – is painted on the inboard vertical stabilizers. The Squadron's tail band is yellow above the Pacific Air Forces (PACAF) insignia. (USAF)

This F-15D-26-MC (79-0014) is assigned to the 2nd FS, 325th FW at Tyndall AFB, Florida. The Eagle is used in the training role, with a secondary role of air defense of the southern United States. The vertical stabilizer has the Air Education and Training Command (AETC) badge below the yellow tail band. The 2nd FS badge is affixed to the air intake. (USAF)

The speed brake is extended soon after GLAMOROUS GLENNIS, an F-15D-38-MC (84-0046) landed at Edwards AFB, California on 14 October 1997. BGen Chuck Yeager flew the Eagle on the 50th anniversary of his breaking the sound barrier in the Bell X-1, also named GLAMOROUS GLENNIS. Conformal Fuel Tanks (CFTs) are mounted on this F-15D. (USAF)

The F-15D GLAMOROUS GLENNIS takes off from Edwards AFB on General Yeager's 50th anniversary flight. Yeager named both this F-15D and the X-1 after his wife. The insignia on the vertical stabilizer commemorated the 50th anniversary of the first supersonic flight. The Eagle is painted in the 'Mod Eagle' camouflage scheme. (USAF)

The F-15D (84-0046) General Yeager flew in 1997 is parked near the Edwards AFB control tower. It is painted in the standard markings, which include a blue tail band with white Xs and trim, the Air Force Flight Test Center (AFFTC) insignia, and the ED tail code. (USAF)

This F-15D (84-0045) flies above its home base of Eglin AFB, Florida. The Eagle was assigned to the 3246th Test Wing (now the 46th Test Wing) of the Air Force Development Test Center. Two AIM-120 AMRAAMs are mounted under the starboard wing. The white tail band has red diamonds and trim, while the Air Force Materiel Command (AFMC) insignia appears below the band. (USAF)

An F-15D-40-MC (85-0134) warms up its engines prior to a training mission at a forward deployed location. The wing flaps are lowered to their maximum 30° setting for pre-flight checks. The flaps are normally lowered for landing and when hydraulic power has bled off after engine shutdown. This Eagle is assigned to the 60th FS, 33rd FW from Eglin AFB and has a red tail band painted above the Air Combat Command (ACC) insignia. (USAF)

F-15E Eagle

In the late 1970s, McDonnell Douglas began converting the second F-15B (71-291) for a company-funded project called Strike Eagle. This project was for a multi-role fighter that would be able to take advantage of the air-to-ground role originally built into the F-15. The idea was to construct a fighter that could fight its way to the target, destroy the intended target and fight its way back home without escort. Secondarily, it was designed to replace the General Dynamics F-111 fighter-bomber.

The Strike Eagle conversion included the installation of the new FAST (Fuel And Sensor Tactical) Pack Conformal Fuel Tanks (CFTs), which McDonnell Douglas developed for the F-15C/D. An improved Hughes AN/APG-63 radar (later to become the AN/APG-70) was installed. The aircraft was also fitted with pods for the Martin Marietta LANTIRN (Low-Altitude Navigation and Targeting Infra-Red, for Night) and FLIR (Forward-Looking Infra-Red) sensors. The front and rear cockpit displays were upgraded, with the back seat configured for a Weapons Systems Officer (WSO). When the conversion was completed, this F-15B was painted in an overall European I 'lizard' camouflage scheme and first flown on 8 July 1980.

The Strike Eagle was built to participate in the USAF's Enhanced Tactical Fighter (ETF) competition. This pitted the Strike Eagle against the General Dynamics F-16XL, an F-16E configured with a highly-swept 'cranked arrow' wing. The Strike Eagle was judged the winner in the competition and was ordered into production as the F-15E Eagle. (The USAF has not formally adopted the name Strike Eagle for the F-15E.)

The first two F-15Es (86-0183/0184) were Block 41 F-15D airframes strengthened to allow an increased maximum take off weight of up to 81,000 pounds (36,741.6 kg). This new airframe reduced internal fuel capacity from 2070 gallons (7835.8 L) to 2019 gallons (7642.7 L). For this reason, all F-15Es are fitted with two CFTs that each hold 728 gallons (2755.8 L) of fuel. The F-15E is also plumbed to carry three 600 gallon (2271.2 L) external fuel tanks – one each under the port and starboard wings and one on the centerline.

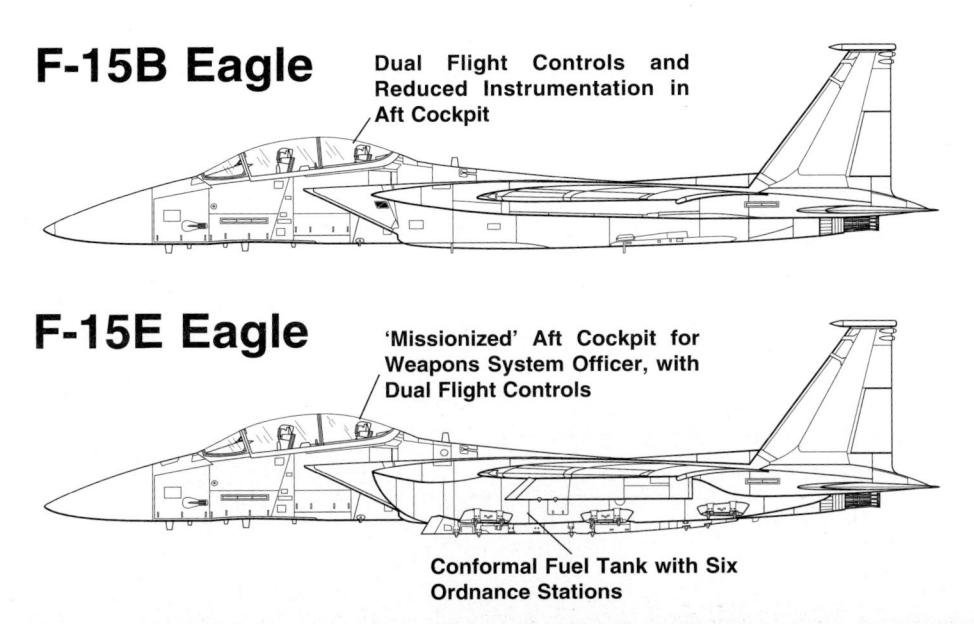

The first F-15E (86-0183) is parked alongside the second F-15B (71-291) outside McDonnell Douglas' St. Louis plant in January of 1987. This F-15B was used in the 'Strike Eagle' tests, which led to the F-15E. The Eagle's engine inlets move from -11° to +4° to provide optimum airflow at all speeds. (McDonnell Douglas)

The first F-15E (86-0183) was an F-15D Block 41 airframe upgraded to E model standards. The aircraft is camouflaged in the overall Gunship Gray (FS36118) scheme, which became standard for all USAF F-15Es. A black eagle motif is painted on the outboard vertical stabilizers. (USAF)

F-15B Eagle
Dual Flight Controls and Reduced Instrumentation in Aft Cockpit

F-15E Eagle
'Missionized' Aft Cockpit for Weapons System Officer, with Dual Flight Controls

Conformal Fuel Tank with Six Ordnance Stations

The F-15E dual-role fighter is armed with one 20mm General Electric M61A1 Vulcan cannon, a six-barrel Gatling-type rotary weapon fed with 450 rounds of ammunition. This gun is mounted in the starboard wing root – the same location as for other Eagles. Up to 24,250 pounds (10,999.8 kg) of external ordnance are carried on six tangential stubs located on the conformal fuel tanks – three per side – and on the two wing pylons. The use of tangential weapons carriage in place of Multiple Ejector Racks (MERs) reduces drag, resulting in a 40 percent increase in the F-15E's range. For the air-to-air role, up to four AIM-9 Sidewinder or four AIM-120 AMRAAM missiles could be carried. In actual service, the F-15E Eagle is usually armed with two AIM-9s, two AIM-120s, and two air-to-ground 'smart bombs.' The latter weapons include the GBU-15 through GBU-23 bombs, depending upon the selected target.

The F-15E is powered by two Pratt & Whitney F-100-PW-229 turbofan engines, which each generate 18,000 pounds of static (dry) pounds of thrust and 29,000 pounds of afterburning (wet) thrust. Full rated speed is Mach 2.5 (1650 mph/2655.3 kmh) at 40,000 feet (12,192 m). The maximum unrefueled range with CFTs is 3570 miles (5745.2 km). Maximum endurance is 15 hours, which is approximately the longest time that an Aircraft Commander (AC, or pilot) and Weapons Systems Officer (WSO) can sit in their ACES II ejection seats. Combat radius with two 600 gallon fuel tanks, a pair of 2000 pound (907.2 kg) bombs, and four air-to-air missiles is 800 miles (1287.4 km). F-15Es are painted overall Gunship Gray (FS36118).

The first two F-15Es (86-0183 and 86-0184) were tested at Edwards AFB, California and Eglin AFB, Florida. Following completion of the flight performance and weapons evaluations, the 'Strike Eagle' was cleared for squadron service. The 425th Tactical Fighter Training Squadron (TFTS) at Luke AFB, Arizona was activated to introduce and train new F-15E crews. The 336th Tactical Fighter Squadron (TFS[1]), 4th Tactical Fighter Wing (TFW[2]) was the first Operational F-15E unit. Forming in 1990 at Seymour Johnson AFB, North Carolina, the 336th TFS 'Rocketeers' trained for just under a year before Operation DESERT SHIELD began in August of 1990. The 336th TFS and its sister squadron the 335th TFS 'Chiefs' were deployed to Kharj Air Base (AB), Saudi Arabia. These units flew hundreds of combat missions during Operation DESERT STORM in early 1991, losing two F-15Es to ground fire. One 335th TFS F-15E made the only 'Strike Eagle' aerial victory of the war on 14 February 1991. It destroyed an Iraqi Hughes Model 500 helicopter by dropping a laser-guided bomb on the helicopter while it was in the air. F-15Es also saw action over Yugoslavia during Operation ALLIED FORCE in 1999 and over Afghanistan during Operation ENDURING FREEDOM in late 2001 and early 2002.

When production is finally completed, Boeing (which acquired McDonnell Douglas in 1998) will have completed 236 F-15E Eagles. The F-15E is assigned to USAF squadrons in the United States and England. The Israel Defense Force/Air Force is receiving 25 examples of an F-15E export version, known as the **F-15I** *Ra'am* (Thunder). The Royal Saudi Air Force has ordered 72 **F-15S** (for Saudi Arabia) aircraft, which are slightly downgraded F-15Es. Its range and payload capabilities put Israel well within its operating radius. The US Government was concerned about the F-15S's performance, but decided that the Iraqi and Iranian threat to Saudi Arabia was greater than concerns about Israel's security. South Korea ordered 40 similar **F-15K**s in April of 2002.

[1] Tactical Fighter Squadrons were renamed Fighter Squadrons in 1992.
[2] The 4th TFW was redesignated the 4th Wing (Wg) in 1992.

The first F-15E (86-0183) makes a test flight from McDonnell Douglas's St. Louis facility in 1986. The aircraft is fitted with LANTIRN navigation and targeting pods under the engine intakes. This Eagle variant is powered by two Pratt & Whitney F-100 PW-229 low bypass turbofan engines, which each produce over 29,000 pounds of thrust. (McDonnell Douglas)

The F-15E prototype is armed with four AIM-7 Sparrow Air-to-Air Missiles (AAMs) for this test flight from Edwards AFB. This Eagle variant retains the full air combat capability of F-15As through Ds alongside its primary air-to-ground role. F-15Es usually carry AIM-9 Sidewinders and AIM-120 AMRAAMs in service, rather than the AIM-7. (USAF)

F-15Es are usually equipped with Lockheed Martin LANTIRN pods under the engine intakes. The AN/AAQ-13 navigation pod under the starboard intake includes a Forward-Looking Infra-Red (FLIR) sensor above a Terrain Following Radar (TFR). The AN/AAQ-14 targeting pod under the port intake features a laser designator for targeting Laser Guided Bombs (LGBs). LANTIRN allows F-15E crews to fly to and from their targets and precisely deliver ordnance in all weather and light conditions. (Lou Drendel)

This F-15E-43-MC (87-0185) flies a training mission from Luke AFB, Arizona. The Eagle is assigned to the 461st TFTS, 405th TTW, which trains F-15E flight crews. It is armed with

A 3246th Test Wing F-15E-42-MC (86-0188) is used to drop test the 4700 pound (2131.9 KG) Paveway III GBU-28 (BLU-113) 'Deep Throat' penetration bomb in 1990. This bomb was used in Iraq in 1991 and in Afghanistan in 2001. The weapon can penetrate the earth up to 100 feet (30.5 M) deep to destroy command and weapons bunkers. The Eagle has an ET tail code and a white tail band with red diamonds and trim. (USAF)

AIM-9 Sidewinders for air-to-air combat and 500 pound Mk 82 'iron' bombs for air-to-ground attacks. (McDonnell Douglas)

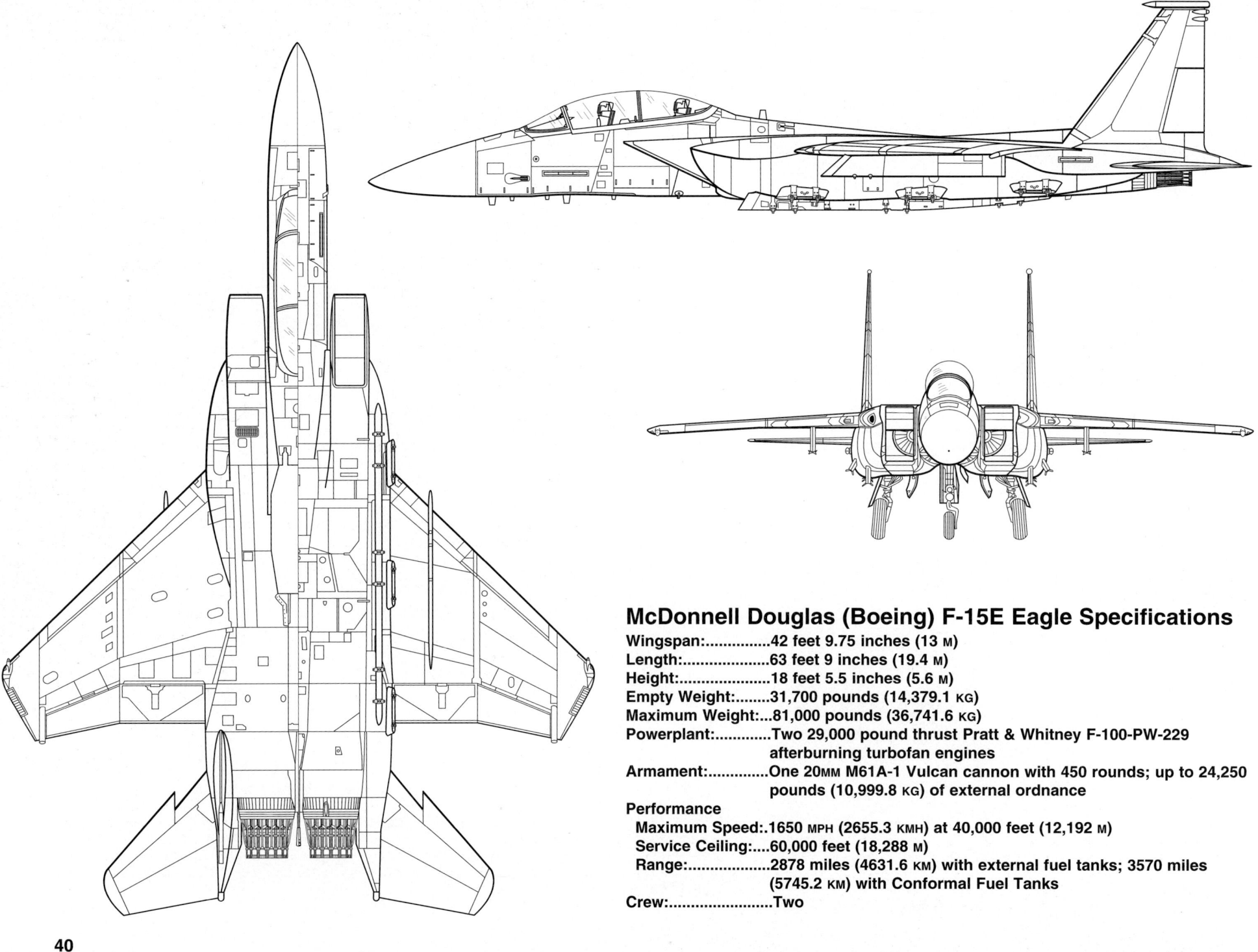

McDonnell Douglas (Boeing) F-15E Eagle Specifications

Wingspan: ....42 feet 9.75 inches (13 м)
Length: ....63 feet 9 inches (19.4 м)
Height: ....18 feet 5.5 inches (5.6 м)
Empty Weight: ....31,700 pounds (14,379.1 кg)
Maximum Weight: ...81,000 pounds (36,741.6 кg)
Powerplant: ....Two 29,000 pound thrust Pratt & Whitney F-100-PW-229 afterburning turbofan engines
Armament: ....One 20мм M61A-1 Vulcan cannon with 450 rounds; up to 24,250 pounds (10,999.8 кg) of external ordnance

Performance
  Maximum Speed:.1650 мрн (2655.3 кмн) at 40,000 feet (12,192 м)
  Service Ceiling:....60,000 feet (18,288 м)
  Range:..................2878 miles (4631.6 км) with external fuel tanks; 3570 miles (5745.2 км) with Conformal Fuel Tanks
Crew: ....Two

An F-15E approaches a tanker for an in-flight refueling. The refueling receptacle door is open on the port wing root. This is the same receptacle found on other Eagle variants. The F-15E has the same external dimensions as the previous F-15A through F-15D Eagles. (USAF)

Both F-15E crewmen sit in ACES II ejection seats. These seats are sometimes covered with removable black fur covers for added comfort on long flights. Circuit breaker panels are located along the starboard wall of the Weapons System Officer (WSO) cockpit. Oxygen and lighting controls are placed atop the starboard console. (Lou Drendel)

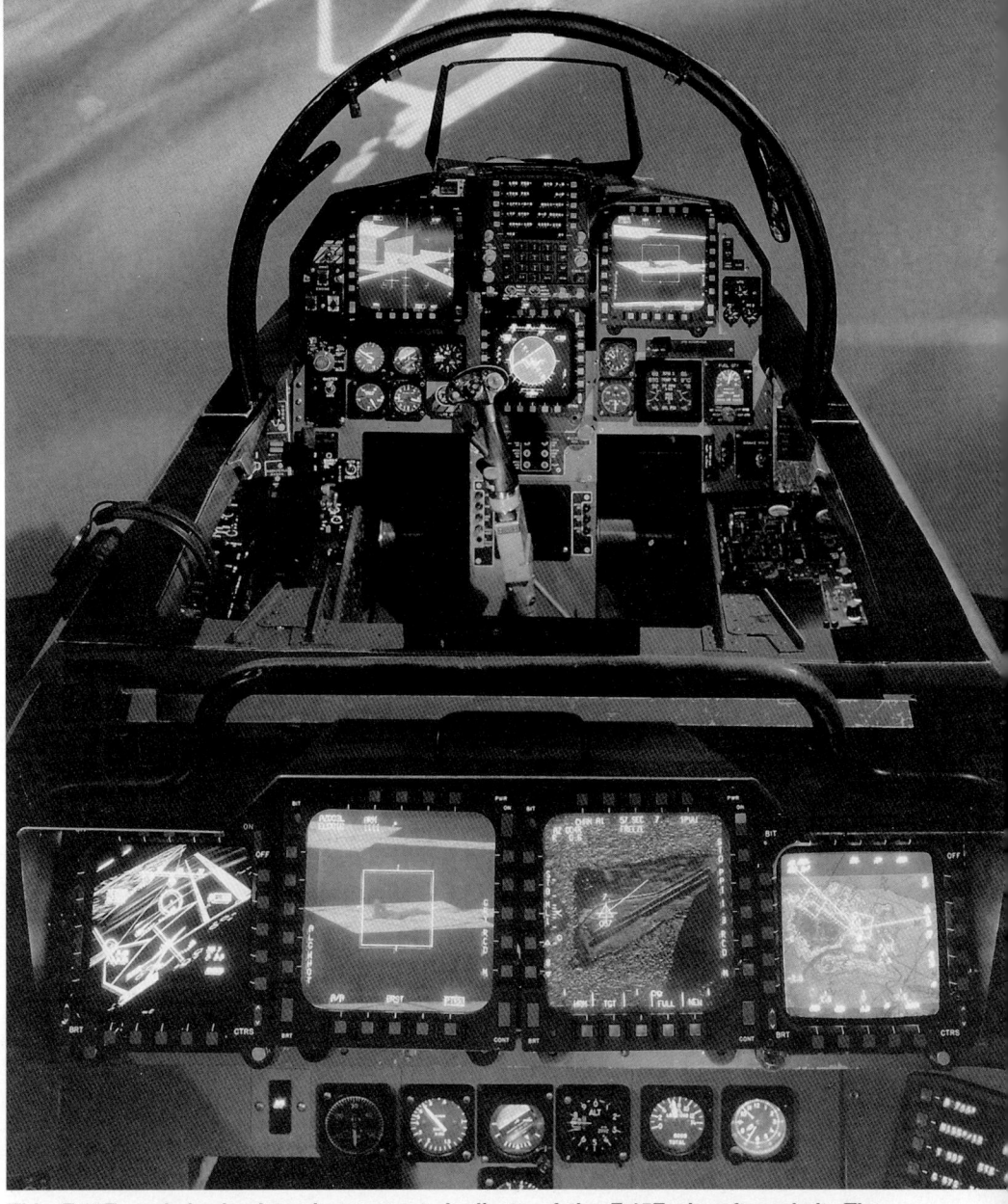

This F-15E cockpit simulator is an exact duplicate of the F-15E aircraft cockpit. The Aircraft Commander (AC, or pilot) sits in front, with the Weapons System Officer (WSO) aft. A wide angle Heads-Up Display (HUD) for displaying key flight information to the AC is mounted atop his instrument panel. This panel is dominated by two Multi-Purpose Displays (MPDs), which show flight data and sensor videos. Two MPDs are located on the WSO's instrument panel and are flanked by two Multi-Purpose Color Displays (MPCDs). (Boeing)

41

A F-15E-44-MC (87-0206) from the 550th FS 'Silver Eagles,' 58th FW sits on the Luke AFB ramp in the early 1990s. The Squadron emblem is affixed to the intake area and the black tail band has SILVER EAGLES and trim in silver. The MXU-648/A equipment pod mounted on the starboard wing pylon has *550th Silver Eagles* painted in black. This pod holds the flight crewmen's personal items while he is deployed away from his home base. (Norris Graser via T. Love)

A 391st FS F-15E (89-0506) drops a pair of 2000 pound Mk 84 'iron' bombs during a test flight. The bombs can be accurately placed on the intended target utilizing the LANTIRN navigation and radar targeting pods under the engine inlets. The 391st FS 'Bold Tigers' was the first F-15E squadron deployed to Central Asia during Operation ENDURING FREEDOM in the fall of 2001. (USAF)

A Luke-based F-15E launches the first flight test of an AGM-65B Maverick air-to-ground missile over the Goldwater Test Range, Arizona in July of 1988. The Maverick was designed as a 'tank buster,' but it can be used for air-to-air missions if required. The F-15E's avionics and electronic suite establish a link with the Maverick missile to locate small tactical targets, including tanks. (McDonnell Douglas)

A F-15E from the 422nd Test and Evaluation Squadron (TES), 57th Wing flies a test mission from Nellis AFB, Nevada. The Eagle is fitted with Mk 7 dispensers (Mk 20 Rockeye cluster bomb units) on the CFT stations. The tail band consists of yellow and black checks and the WA tail code and unit designator are black with white shadowing. (USAF)

A 334th FS F-15E drops a 3000 pound (1360.8 KG) AGM-130 rocket assisted bomb. It is an adverse weather weapon that utilizes a GBU-15 bomb, a seeker head from an AGM-65 Maverick, and a 2000 pound (907.2 KG) Mk 84 warhead. The AGM-130 interfaces with the F-15E's navigation, avionics, and radar suite to locate and destroy the intended target. This weapon has a range of 40 miles (64.4 KM). (USAF)

A 550th TFTS F-15E-43-MC (87-0187) drops twelve 500 pound Mk 82 bombs on the Goldwater Test Range in June of 1989. These weapons were released from tangentially mounted pylons fitted to the Conformal Fuel Tanks (CFTs). Markings on the vertical stabilizer indicate this F-15E is the 'flagship' of the 550th Aircraft Maintenance Unit (AMU), which coordinates aircraft maintenance for the 550th TFTS. (McDonnell Douglas)

The Aircraft Commander and his Weapons Systems Officer (WSO) of this F-15E (89-0504) go over the mission profile before taking off at Tyndall AFB, Florida in 1992. The Eagle is assigned to the 336th FS (formerly TFS) 'Rocketeers,' 4th Wing from Seymour Johnson AFB. The tail band is (from front) yellow, green, and blue stripe, while a rendition of the Wright Flyer is painted on the inboard vertical stabilizer surfaces. (Al Adcock)

The 'flagship' of the 90th FS, 3rd Wing from Elmendorf AFB is this F-15E (90-0233). The Eagle flies over the Nevada desert during a RED FLAG exercise in 1999. Nellis AFB hosts the RED FLAGs to test and improve on inter-service and inter-country cooperation against air and ground 'threats.' (USAF)

A F-15E-45-MC (88-1684) of the 334th FS, 4th Wing takes the high point so another F-15E can refuel from a Boeing KC-135R Stratotanker. The Wing is based at Seymour Johnson AFB, North Carolina and was the first operational F-15E unit. The near F-15E's speed brake is unpainted – believed to be a replacement – and the tail band is red with white trim. (USAF)

A maintenance crew changes the port F100-PW-229 engine of an F-15E (91-0314) at Royal Air Force (RAF) Lakenheath, England. This Eagle is the 'flagship' of the 494th FS, 48th FW at Lakenheath and is normally flown by the Squadron Commander. The F-15's two engines can be changed in 30 minutes. (USAF)

Two F-15Es assigned to the 391st FS, 366th Wing fly past the Pyramids of Giza, Egypt. The Eagles deployed from Mountain Home AFB, Idaho to Egypt for the joint US/Egyptian BRIGHT STAR military exercises. The 366th Wing is tasked with rapidly projecting US air power anywhere in the world. (USAF)

A 391st FS F-15E maneuvers under a McDonnell Douglas KC-10A Extender tanker to take on fuel over Afghanistan during Operation ENDURING FREEDOM. The F-15E is armed with two AIM-120 AMRAAMs and two AIM-9 Sidewinders, with one 2000 pound GBU-10 Paveway laser guided bomb on the starboard wing pylon. A 600 gallon (2271.2 L) fuel tank is fitted to the port wing pylon. (USAF)

An F-15E (91-0316) from the 494th FS, 48th FW launches from RAF Lakenheath for Central Asia to support Operation ENDURING FREEDOM in late 2001. The Eagle is equipped with three 600 gallon fuel tanks and it carries no external armament. The Squadron's tail band is red outlined in white. The 48th FW is the only F-15E unit based outside the Continental US (CONUS). (USAF)

A forward deployed F-15E-43-MC (87-0173) from the 391st FS taxies out to an active runway prior to taking off on a mission over Afghanistan in 2001. This Eagle is armed with 2000 pound GBU-27 laser guided bombs and AIM-120 AMRAAM air-to-air missiles. The tail band is orange with black tiger stripes. The 322nd Air Expeditionary Group controlled the 391st FS during Operation ENDURING FREEDOM. (USAF)

An F-15A Eagle (683) taxis at Tel Nof AB in central Israel. This aircraft is assigned to 133 'Twin Tails' Squadron, Israel Defense Force/Air Force (IDF/AF) at Tel Nof. Israeli F-15As and F-15Bs are each called *Baz* (Falcon) and are camouflaged in Compass Ghost Gray, with the Squadron insignia painted on the upper vertical stabilizer. (IDF/AF)

Two F-15 aircraft from 106 'Second Eagle' Squadron fly a Combat Air Patrol from Tel Nof. The near aircraft is an F-15C (840) named *Skyblazer*, which is credited with downing six Syrian aircraft. Flying with 840 is an F-15D (957). Both Eagles – each dubbed *Akef* (Buzzard) by the IDF/AF – are armed with Israeli-made Python 3 heat-seeking Air-to-Air Missiles (AAMs). (IDF/AF)

Foreign Operators

Many air forces evaluated the new F-15, including those of Iran, West Germany, Canada, Great Britain, and France. It was the Israel Defense Force/Air Force (IDF/AF) that became the first foreign Eagle customer when they began receiving the F-15A in December of 1976. These aircraft were sold under Peace Fox I, a US Foreign Military Sales (FMS) program. The IDF/AF's 133 'Twin Tail' Squadron at Tel Nof Air Base (AB) in central Israel received the first four F-15As (72-0116/0118 and 72-0120). These aircraft came from pre-production stocks and were camouflaged in the Compass Ghost Gray scheme of Light Ghost Gray (FS36375) and Dark Ghost Gray (FS36320). These initial aircraft were soon followed by Peace Fox II, with 19 more F-15As (76-1505/1523) and two TF-15As (F-15Bs, 76-1524/1525) delivered to Israel. The IDF/AF calls the F-15A/B the *Baz* (Falcon).

The IDF/AF formed 106 Squadron, also at Tel Nof, especially to operate the F-15C/D in 1981. FMS program Peace Fox III resulted in the delivery of F-15C/D aircraft, locally called the *Akef* (Buzzard). The US delivered 18 F-15Cs (80-0122/0130 and 83-0054/0062) and eight F-15Ds (80-0131/0136 and 83-0063/0064) to the IDF/AF, which supplemented their F-15A/B fighters.

In 1994, the Israeli government ordered a version of the F-15E designated the F-15I (I for Israel). The first F-15I (94-0287) was delivered to the IDF/AF in 1998 and called the *Ra'am* (Thunder). The F-15I features a downgraded AN/APG-63 radar and many Israeli-made electronic components. F-15I upper surfaces are camouflaged in Tan (FS33531), Brown (FS30219), and Light Green (FS34424), while undersurfaces are Light Ghost Gray (FS36375). This scheme is painted on the IDF/AF's McDonnell Douglas F-4 and Douglas A-4 Skyhawk ground attack aircraft. The F-15I serves with the 69 Squadron (the 'Hammer Squadron') at Hatzerim AB, in south central Israel.

IDF/AF Eagles first saw action against Syrian aircraft over Lebanon in 1979. Israeli F-15 pilots have a perfect record of over 40 victories and no defeats. An F-15C named *Skyblazer* (s/n 840) claimed six Syrian aircraft destroyed. The IDF/AF arms its F-15s with AIM-9 Sidewinders and Israeli manufactured Rafael Shafrir and Python heat-seeking air-to-air missiles.

In the mid 1970s, the Imperial Government of Japan began searching for a replacement for its Lockheed F-104J Starfighters and chose the F-15 following evaluation flights of the Eagle and other contenders. After contract agreements, it was decided that the Mitsubishi Heavy Industries would construct the F-15 in Nagoya, Japan. McDonnell Douglas built the first two single seat **F-15J**s (J for Japan) under Project Peace Eagle. The F-15J is similar to the F-15C, but lacks some Electronic Countermeasures (ECM) equipment and nuclear weapons capability. The first two F-15Js were assigned the USAF serial numbers 79-0280 and 79-0281. When they entered Japan Air Self-Defense Force (JASDF) service, they were reserialed 02-8801 and 02-8802. Mitsubishi assembled the next eight F-15Js from knockdown components built by McDonnell Douglas in St. Louis and shipped to Japan. The Japanese then began license construction of the remaining F-15Js. A similar agreement was reached with the two-seat F-15DJ, with McDonnell Douglas building the first 12 aircraft and Mitsubishi constructing the 16 remaining F-15DJs ordered by Japan.

The JASDF operate 191 F-15J/DJ aircraft (including 177 built by Mitsubishi) in seven front line squadrons, two training squadrons, and one aggressor unit. Japanese F-15s are painted in a gray on gray camouflage scheme similar to the USAF Compass Ghost Gray scheme. The exception is the *Hiko Kyodo-tai* (Aggressor Group) based at Nyutabaru, whose F-15DJs are painted various schemes of blue, green, and gray.

The Royal Saudi Air Force (RSAF) began receiving its first F-15Cs in 1981. This sale – under the FMS project Peace Sun – caused quite a stir in the US Congress, as that august body has much support for Israel. The delivery took place after the Saudis assured the US that the F-15Cs were only going to be used for defensive purposes. The order also included 16 two-seat F-15Ds for training and familiarization purposes. All RSAF F-15C/Ds are equipped to carry the Conformal Fuel Tanks (CFTs), but it is not known if CFTs were delivered to Saudi Arabia as of 2002. The F-15C drew first blood on 5 June 1984, when two Saudi F-15Cs each shot down an intruding Iranian F-4E Phantom over the Persian Gulf. This engagement occurred during the Iran-Iraq War of 1980-88.

The RSAF F-15C/Ds serve with 5 Squadron at King Fahd AB, 6 Squadron at King Khalid AB, and 13 Squadron at King Abdul Aziz AB. There are now over 100 F-15C/D Eagles serving with the RSAF. A condition of the sale provided that no more than 60 RSAF F-15s could be in the country at any one time. This provision was waived when Iraqi ruler Saddam Hussein sent his forces to invade neighboring Kuwait on 2 August 1990. The US sent at least 25 (and perhaps as many as 40) F-15Cs to Saudi Arabia to help the Allied Coalition Forces defend the oil rich country. Saddam's forces were ejected from Kuwait during Operation DESERT STORM in early 1991. RSAF Captain Ayehid Salah al-Shamrani of 13 Squadron made the only non-US kills of the war when he destroyed two Iraqi Mirage F-1EQ fighters with AIM-9 Sidewinders on 24 January 1991. Saudi Arabia has ordered 72 F-15S Eagles, which are slightly downgraded F-15Es. These aircraft will augment the RSAF's Panavia Tornado strike aircraft.

A number of other countries are interested in obtaining the F-15 Eagle for their air forces as of 2002. Greece's Hellenic Air Force is requesting up to 60 aircraft from the USAF inventory, once the Lockheed Martin/Boeing F-22 Raptor begins to replace the F-15 in front line service. In April of 2002, South Korea ordered 40 F-15Ks, another export version of the F-15E. The Republic of Singapore Air Force has flown demonstration flights in the F-15E and is interested in ordering a version of this dual-role fighter.

Four 133 Squadron F-15As fly over the historic fortress of Masada in 1978. Jewish rebels held out in this fortress near the Dead Sea against Roman forces in 73-74 A.D., before the defenders committed suicide rather than be captured. Israeli F-15As through Ds are painted in the Compass Ghost Gray scheme. (McDonnell Douglas)

An F-15I *Ra'am* (Thunder) makes a test flight over the United States in 1998. It retained its USAF serial number (98-0287) prior to delivery to the IDF/AF. The F-15I is an electronically downgraded version of the F-15E flown by 69 'Hammer' Squadron at Hatzerim in south central Israel. The *Ra'am* is camouflaged in Tan (FS33531), Light Green (FS34424), and Brown (FS30219) over Light Ghost Gray (FS36375). (IDF/AF)

Three 133 Squadron F-15As – 520 leading 684 and 669 – fly over Jerusalem. Israeli F-15A/Bs have white eagle heads painted on black bands on the inboard vertical stabilizers. Three Syrian 'kill' marks are painted on the nose of 684. (IDF/AF)

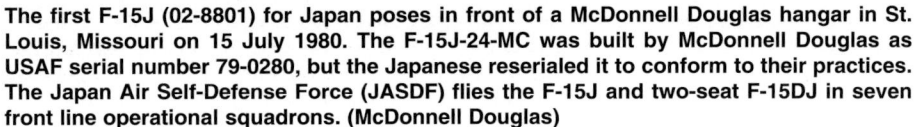

The first F-15J (02-8801) for Japan poses in front of a McDonnell Douglas hangar in St. Louis, Missouri on 15 July 1980. The F-15J-24-MC was built by McDonnell Douglas as USAF serial number 79-0280, but the Japanese reserialed it to conform to their practices. The Japan Air Self-Defense Force (JASDF) flies the F-15J and two-seat F-15DJ in seven front line operational squadrons. (McDonnell Douglas)

An F-15J (62-8872) of 204 *Hikotai*, 7 *Kokudan* flies past Mount Fuji. The Squadron is based at Hyakuri on the main Japanese Island of Honshu. This Eagle is fitted with three 600 gallon fuel tanks and displays the Squadron's eagle's head on all vertical tail surfaces. (JASDF)

Mitsubishi assembled this F-15J-25 (22-8810) in Japan from components manufactured by McDonnell Douglas in the United States. This F-15J serves with the 304 *Hikotai* (Squadron), 8 *Kokudan* (Wing) at Tsuiki Air Base on the southern Japanese Island of Kyushu. The Squadron insignia is painted on the upper vertical stabilizer. (JASDF)

An F-15J (32-8824) climbs alongside another Eagle after taking off for a Combat Air Patrol (CAP) over the Sea of Japan. These F-15Js are assigned to 201 *Hikotai*, 2 *Kokudan* at Chitose on the northern Japanese Island of Hokkaido. This Squadron's insignia is a bear's head, which is painted on the vertical stabilizers. (JASDF)

A specially painted 204 *Hikotai* F-15J (42-8828) prepares to land during an air show in Japan. The landing gear is extended and the speed brake is fully deployed at a 45° angle. The yellow, red, white, and blue eagle scheme celebrated the Squadron's 30th Anniversary in 1991. (JASDF)

This F-15DJ (82-8865) is one of six two-seat Eagles assigned to the *Hiko Kyodo-tai* (Aggressor Group) at Nyutabaru. This unit acts as 'enemy' fighters against JASDF aircraft in training exercises. The *Hiko Kyodo-tai*'s F-15DJs have colored bands painted over their Compass Ghost Gray finish; green in the case of 82-8865. (JASDF)

Two F-15C Eagles (1306 and 1311) of 13 Squadron, Royal Saudi Air Force (RSAF) fly a Combat Air Patrol (CAP) mission in 1988. This unit is based at King Abdul Aziz AB in Dhahran, in northeast Saudi Arabia. These Eagles are armed with AIM-7 Sparrow and AIM-9 Sidewinder air-to-air missiles. Each fighter has a 600 gallon fuel tank fitted to the centerline stores station. (McDonnell Douglas)

A RSAF F-15C (1311) launches an AIM-7 Sparrow air-to-air missile during a test flight from Tyndall AFB, Florida. A 13 Squadron RSAF F-15C downed two Iraqi Air Force Mirage F1s on a CAP during Operation DESERT STORM in January of 1991. RSAF F-15C/Ds are camouflaged in the Compass Ghost gray scheme, with green markings. (McDonnell Douglas)

More US Combat Aircraft

1045 P-51 Mustang

1067 P-47 Thunderbolt

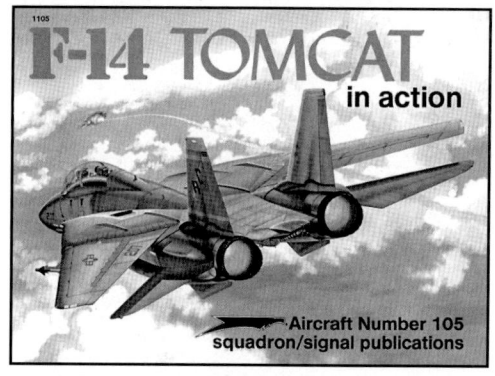

1105 F-14 Tomcat

1115 F-117 Stealth

1140 F3H Demon

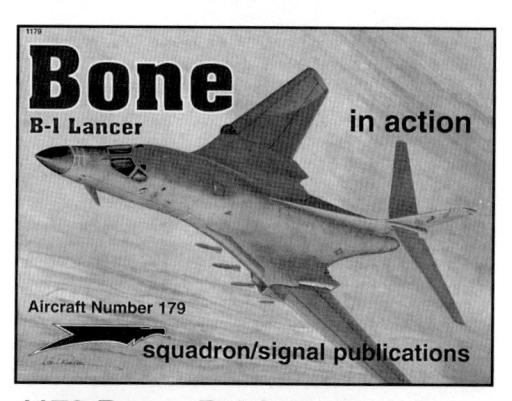

1179 Bone: B-1 Lancer

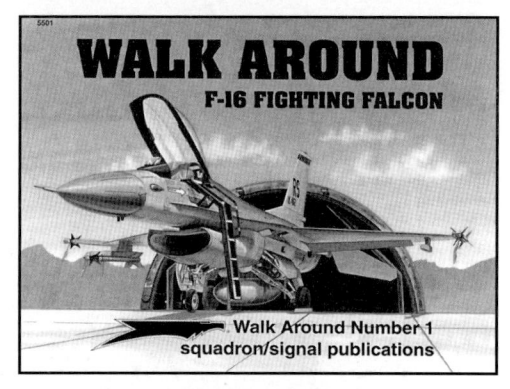

5501 F-16 Walk Around

5523 F-105 Walk Around

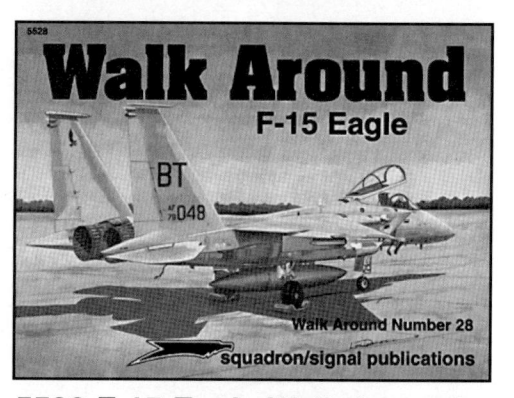

5528 F-15 Eagle Walk Around

from squadron/signal publications